How to Get Through

THE DARK NIGHT

OF THE SOUL

Overcoming Spiritual Depression During Awakening

Sophia Persephone Ambrose

Copyright 2023 Sophia Persephone Ambrose

All Rights Reserved.

First Transcended Owl Press Edition 2023

No part of this book may be reproduced by any mechanical, photographic, or electronic process, or in the form of a phonographic recording; nor may it be stored in a retrieval system, transmitted, or otherwise be copied for public or private use—other than for "fair use" as brief quotations embodied in articles and reviews—without prior written permission of the publisher.

The author of this book does not dispense medical advice or prescribe the use of any technique as a form of treatment for any physical, emotional, or medical problems without the advice of a physician, either directly or indirectly. The intent of the author is only to offer information of a general nature to help you in your quest for emotional and spiritual well-being and along your path to spiritual enlightenment. In the event you use any of the information in this book for yourself, the author and the publisher assume no responsibility for your actions.

Visit the author's website at https://sophiapersephone.com
Find the author on Instagram, YouTube, and TikTok at:
sophiapersephoneawakening
ISBN for electronic edition, e-pub format: 978-1-7393354-0-3
ISBN for print format: 978-1-7393354-1-0

About the Author

Sophia Persephone Ambrose is a writer, artist, and spiritual teacher from London, England. She has completed her spiritual awakening and is now fully integrated with her higher self, Sophia, whose name she has adopted. During her awakening, Sophia Persephone learned how our universe works, the nature of the soul and its relationship with us as human beings, as well as how to navigate through the spiritual awakening process from beginning to end. She also discovered that part of her purpose in this life is to share the information given to her and to help others through their own awakenings. Sophia Persephone's spiritual awakening has transformed her life and she is now lucky enough to live in the most beautiful part of Southern Spain, spending her time painting and writing.

For Sophia, Freya, and Om, thank you for your unwavering faith, love, and support.

"Peace can only come as a natural consequence of universal enlightenment."

—Nikola Tesla

Preface

In 2021 I spent four seemingly endless months feeling as though something vital had been cut out of me. I was fragile, irritable, frustrated, and angry. I had no interest in anything. I spent all day in bed watching Netflix. Life seemed meaningless and I wondered, "what's the point?" What made this strange depression—that had descended suddenly, without obvious cause—particularly difficult to bear, was that it arrived after a protracted period of intense connection to my higher self and guides.

For a long time, my awakening journey was euphoric. I felt completely in tune with the universe and finally understood the meaning of the words, "we are all one". I was speaking with my higher self and guides daily and was 'in flow'. Then, out of the blue, nothing. All communication was cut off, overnight. I later learned I had entered the spiritual Dark Night of the Soul, a vital stage of the awakening journey and a spiritual rite of passage.

I failed to get through the Dark Night of the Soul that time. Instead I slid backwards along the spiritual awakening continuum and exited the Dark Night the way I had come in. Once communication with my team was restored, they taught me a raft of spiritual 'protocols' for my next attempt. Using these protocols meant I traversed my second Dark Night in just three weeks.

The difference in the two experiences was extreme. Knowing what to do meant I could focus on 'curing' my spiritual depression in a practical way. I had confidence I was taking the steps I needed to get through to the other side of the Dark Night of the Soul. Yet when I had previously researched on the internet I had found no information of this kind. It was one of the major reasons I failed to overcome the Dark Night on my first attempt—there was no practical guidance available. "What about all the other poor souls around the World going through this difficult stage of awakening?" I wondered, "How will they know what to do?"

It was then that my higher self, Sophia, asked me to write this book. By sharing everything I had learned during my own Dark Night of the Soul, I saw I could help others successfully get through their own Dark Nights. This is one of my missions in this lifetime.

My other purpose is to share everything my team has taught me about how our universe works and help pave the way for the "New Science". As well as revealing the mechanics of the spiritual awakening journey, my team has shared with me a vast quantity of information about our universe. They have given me the answers to weighty questions such as: "What are we?", "Why are we here?", and "What is the plan for the Earth?".

So, while this book predominantly deals with the Dark Night of the Soul and how to get through it (there are two types of Dark Night, both of which I explain in full), I also share some of these answers with you. Without this context it's impossible to understand the Dark Night and the wider spiritual awakening journey.

We are right on the cusp of the new age of enlightenment. The process of mass awakening has already started and will accelerate rapidly. Unless people like you have the information and tools you need to complete the spiritual awakening journey, there is a danger the global enlightenment project will fail. In addition, tough times are coming. Our planet is about to enter a turbulent period of its history. It will be harder for people to complete their awakening journeys without the guidance provided in these pages. I wrote this book so that you have all the tools you need to reach your full awakening potential, whatever the circumstances, and so that together we can transform life on Earth.

Table of Contents

About the Author iii
Preface vi
Introduction 1

Part I: 3
What is the Dark Night of the Soul and Why Does it Happen? .. 3

Chapter 1—Context: Why Are We Here, and What is "Here" Anyway? 4
The Nature of Our Universe 4
The Game of Life 5
The Mass Global Awakening 6
The First Wave of Awakeners 8
A Definition of "Spiritual Awakening" 9

Chapter 2—How the Dark Night of the Soul Relates to Chakra Health 12
The Dark Night of the Soul in Religious Tradition 12
Chakric Constriction and The Dark Night of the Soul 13
The Function of the Chakras 14
A Description of Each of the Seven Chakras 16

Chapter 3—The Two Types of the Dark Night of the Soul 22
The Growth-Oriented Dark Night of the Soul 22
The Symptoms of the Growth-Oriented Dark Night of the Soul 26
How Long Does the Growth-Oriented Dark Night of the Soul Last? 27
The Purpose of the Growth-Oriented Dark Night of the Soul .. 28
The Spiritual Dark Night of the Soul 28

The Symptoms of the Spiritual Dark Night of the Soul 30
How Long Does the Spiritual Dark Night of the Soul Last? 34
The Purpose of the Spiritual Dark Night of the Soul 35
Identifying Which Type of Dark Night You're In 40
Which Type of Dark Night Are You in?—Questionnaire. 41

Chapter 4—The Other Side of The Dark Night of the Soul .. 44
Reaching The Other Side of the Growth-Oriented Dark Night of the Soul 44
Reaching the Other Side of the Spiritual Dark Night of the Soul 45
Summary of Benefits 62

Part II: 64
Protocols for Getting Through a Dark Night of the Soul 64

Chapter 5—An Overview of the Protocols 65
Introduction 65
The Six Categories of Protocols 66

Chapter 6—Mindset Protocols 68
Protocol 1: Accept the Situation You Are In 68
Protocol 2: Remember What Is Waiting for You on the Other Side 69
Protocol 3: Be Kind to Yourself 70
Protocol 4: Rest—a Lot 71
Protocol 5: Take One Day at a Time 72
Protocol 6: Decide to Succeed 73

Chapter 7—Healthy Living Protocols 76
Protocol 7: Get Rid of Addictive Substances 76
Protocol 8: Eat a "Spiritual" Diet 80
Protocol 9: Take Supplements 84
Protocol 10: Spend Time in Nature 85
Protocol 11: Spend Time in Water 86

Protocol 12: Head for the Sun 87
Protocol 13: Practice Yoga and Other
Forms of Gentle Exercise 88
Protocol 14: Get a Pet 90
Protocol 15: Investigate Psychedelic Therapies 91

Chapter 8—Spiritual Practice Protocols 94
Protocol 16: Meditate Daily 94
Protocol 17: Try Self-Hypnosis 98
Protocol 18: Teach Yourself to Lucid Dream 99
Protocol 19: Use Energy Clearing Exercises 101
Protocol 20: Practice Grounding 103
Protocol 21: Practice Gratitude 105
Protocol 22: Affirmations and Visualizations 108
Protocol 23: Pray/Ask the Universe for Help 111
Protocol 24: Talk to Your Team Even If
You Feel They're Not Listening 113
Protocol 25: Connect with Other People 114

Chapter 9—Self-Development Protocols 116
Protocol 26: Keep a Diary or Blog 117
Protocol 27: Research 118
Protocol 28: Do Your Inner Work 119
Protocol 29: Consider Therapy 122
Protocol 30: Find a Coach or Teacher 123
Protocol 31: Get Rid of Bad Habits 123
Protocol 32: Carry Out a Life Audit 128
Protocol 33: Make a Plan 130
Protocol 34: Find Your Purpose 131

Chapter 10—Creative Protocols 136
Protocol 35: Get Creating 137
Protocol 36: Immerse Yourself in Music 138

Chapter 11—Giving Back Protocols 143

Protocol 37: Do Things for Others *143*
Protocol 38: Find Ways to be Useful *147*
Protocol 39: Communicate Your Experience *148*
Protocol 40: Celebrate! *150*

Chapter 12—How to Incorporate the Protocols into Your Life **152**
Incorporating the Protocols into the Growth-Oriented Dark Night—Introduction *152*
Growth-Oriented Dark Night—Incorporating Protocols: Stage 1 .... *153*
Growth-Oriented Dark Night—Incorporating Protocols: Stage 2 .... *154*
Growth-Oriented Dark Night—Incorporating Protocols: Stage 3 .... *155*
Growth-Oriented Dark Night—What to Do Once You've Completed These Stages *156*
Incorporating the Protocols into the Spiritual Dark Night—Introduction *156*
Spiritual Dark Night—Incorporating Protocols: Stage 1 ...... *157*
Spiritual Dark Night—Incorporating Protocols: Stage 2 ...... *158*
Spiritual Dark Night—Incorporating Protocols: Stage 3 ...... *159*
Spiritual Dark Night—What to Do Once You're Out the Other Side *160*
Incorporating the Protocols—Conclusion *160*

Afterword **162**
A Message from Sophia *162*

A Request from the Author **163**
Glossary **165**
Recommended Reading **171**
Bibliography **177**

Introduction

This book is designed to shine a new light on spiritual depression, why it happens, and what to do about it—topics which are barely understood today. The aim is to provide information and tools to help anyone get through a Dark Night of the Soul, in an action-oriented, practical way.

I have structured the book in two parts. The first provides the context of the human spiritual journey and gives the answers to big, important questions such as: What are we? What is this World we find ourselves in? Why are we here? Why are people waking up now? It also zooms in on the causes of spiritual depression, examines the two types of Dark Night of the Soul, and explains why the spiritual Dark Night is a vital part of the awakening journey. I also reveal what lies on the other side of the Dark Night and why you should commit to pushing on through (spoiler alert: it's wonderful).

The second part of the book is designed to provide the toolkit you need to get through a spiritual depression. These tools are helpful at any stage of the awakening journey, inside and outside of a Dark Night of the Soul. I share the specific protocols I was taught by my higher self, Sophia, my primary guides, Om and Freya, and other members of the Council of Light. (The Council of Light is the organisation which oversees our world and is steered by ten of the oldest souls in our universe.) I also provide specific exercises you can do while reading this book to help you in your journey. Having coached others through their own Dark Nights I'm confident the methods my guides taught me will work for everyone. Adopting even ten percent of what I teach in this book could transform your life.

Please note: I wrote this book with the help of my spiritual team—Sophia, Om, and Freya—during multiple channelling sessions. Much of this information is brand new and currently only exists in this book. Where possible, I have attempted to validate my team's teachings with additional research, but I haven't always been able to. However, I have compared my own experience and the things I've been told with the journeys and learnings of other awakeners I've coached. The correlations are clear. In addition, the seeds of the "New Science" are visibly sprouting all around. In my extensive reading in this area, I've found nothing to contradict the information I've received from Sophia, Om, and Freya.

If you're sceptical (and it's right to question everything, that's how we learn), then I advise you to "turn within". If you work on developing communication with your own team, they will be able to verify or contradict the information contained in these pages. Perhaps they will add to it. In any of these cases, I would be interested to hear what they have to say, so please get in touch: (sophiaambroseowlproject@gmail.com).

If you're reading this book because you're going through a Dark Night of the Soul, take heart. It's tough, demoralizing, and can feel as though it will last forever. It won't. You can and will get through to the other side if you follow the advice in this book. You are a glorious, creative, bright, intelligent, immortal soul, who can overcome anything. All the power of the universe is waiting for you on the other side of the sunless canyon known as the Dark Night of the Soul. This book is your bridge.

Part I:

What is the Dark Night of the Soul and Why Does it Happen?

Chapter 1—Context: Why Are We Here, and What is "Here" Anyway?

The Nature of Our Universe

To understand the context of the mass, global awakening, which is just now beginning on Earth, it's helpful to know what Earth is. Not just our planet in fact, but our entire universe. At its essence, it's a learning environment which we, as souls, have created ourselves. Our born purpose is to gather knowledge and use it to improve both our own universe and the five parallel universes we're connected to. Incarnating on Earth is one way we do this.

This is one of the reasons that life on this planet is so difficult. We give ourselves challenges to overcome so we can learn more profoundly. It helps us evolve at both an individual and collective level. This desire to learn is also the reason we are birthed into a human body with "amnesia." We deliberately forget all we know about what we are and why we're here, and lose access to the vast reserves of knowledge stored in the universal database—the Akashic records. We travel from human life to human life, in the spirit of learning—in other words, we reincarnate.

The process of spiritual awakening restores this information. Once again we understand that we're immortal souls, incarnated in a human body for this lifetime. We also regain some access to the Akashic records. The extent of this differs from individual to individual, depending on their innate abilities and their mission in this lifetime. Each of us incarnates with a plan, even though we have forgotten it on arrival. That's why we have guides, to try to keep us on course. It's also the reason some events or meetings seem 'fated,' they were planned long before we were even born. The important question at this time is why? Why are we regaining this knowledge now? The answer is, it's part of "The Game of Life".

The Game of Life

Souls are highly creative, intelligent beings. Not only that but they also live for ever, so there's a lot of time to fill. Because of this, and for our own amusement, we have 'gamified' our experience on Earth. As with any game, there are rules. One of these rules is that our guides can rarely give us explicit direction. That's why signs and messages can often seem so oblique. If our teams in the higher dimensions could just tell us what to do, that would reduce the fun of the game and also our chances of learning.

Another feature of the Game of Life, as with many games, is that there are two teams (it's a simplification, but you get the idea). These teams have opposing missions (and sub-missions—it's a tangled web!). This creates something to push against and makes the game more enjoyable. The over-arching mission for the Earth right now is global enlightenment. In "Soul World" (the name I use for the higher dimensions), this goal of enlightenment for the Earth is called a "story waypoint". We have to reach this waypoint to move on to the next phase of the game. However, there are those whose mission it is to become enlightened, via spiritual awakening, and those whose mission it is to prevent it. If you're reading this book you are almost certainly in the former camp.

So the answer to "why now?" is quite simply, it's time. In fact, each of our parallel universes reached this waypoint some time ago and are romping along to the next chapter. It's testament to the skill of the incumbent team (the "establishment" if you like) that it's taking us so long to get there. There's no judgement attached to this protracted journey—remember, we have all the time in the World. In fact it's a point of significant interest for the wider soul community, especially as it gives an expanded opportunity for learning, our primary purpose as souls. The "Earth Project," led by Sophia and Om, senior members of the Council of Light, is the greatest show in the universe right now.

The Mass Global Awakening

Imagine we live in a universe that comprises thirteen dimensions (we do). Imagine also that the higher dimensions are vastly more advanced than we are here on Earth (they are). In fact, the highest dimensions are eight thousand years ahead of us in the future, although "future" is a fluid concept once you understand how time works—but that is a subject for another book.

So, the society of Soul World, while it shares characteristics with our Earth society, has shed the more primitive features we still live with on this planet today. Hate, fear, war, greed—in the higher planes we have eliminated these. This is because each dimension has gone through a collective spiritual awakening, and souls on those levels have attained enlightenment. In fact, the way of life in the higher dimensions is the way of "Zen." That will be true for the Earth too, years in our future.

Enlightenment is being rolled out through each of the dimensions, from top to bottom (these were previous story waypoints in the Game of Life). Each dimension becomes more physical as you descend. Earth, inhabiting the third dimension from the bottom, is one of the most physical and therefore we will take longer to attain mass enlightenment, because it's more difficult to effect change in a dense, material realm. However, it's happening.

In fact, if you look closely (and not even that closely), you can see the signs all around you. The process of global spiritual awakening for the Earth started in the sixties but failed to gather momentum.

Think, for example, of the enormous impact the Beatles had. These were four highly evolved beings who came here to show us a different way of thinking and living: *the way of love.* Sad to say, their ideas (and those of others at the time) did not take hold in wider society. So, we have begun anew, this time with an influx of highly evolved souls who have incarnated on the Earth with the express intention of "waking up" and lighting the way for others. If you're reading this book, it's likely you are such a soul, and your team led you to these pages so you could complete your awakening.

The Plan for Earth

I learned many wonderful things during my own spiritual awakening, but one of the most gratifying was to discover the existence of the enlightenment waypoint for Earth. In other words, there's a "plan." More accurately, you would call it an "intention," because the free will accorded to human beings makes it difficult to make an exact plan. That's part of the fun. The intention is "Nirvana"—the relinquishing of attachment to suffering and desire. We're a thousand years from total enlightenment and the state of Nirvana, however the next two hundred years or so will see massive, incremental change for the better.

With enlightenment comes the shedding of the "Ego" and the letting go of all things that cause hurt and pain in the world. We regain full comprehension of ourselves as souls and remember there is a different way to live, in harmony and with equality, as in the higher dimensions. With enlightenment comes a transformed society, an end to suffering, and a new era of peace. So, if you're in this early wave of awakeners, congratulations. You're part of something monumental which has been intended since the beginning of time.

Things will accelerate in the coming months and years. If you're awakening, you will notice others awakening around you. In fact, I see people all the time who are on the journey, but haven't realized it yet. They will soon have their epiphany as I did (if they require one). A crucial factor in our successful mass awakening is getting through the Dark Night of the Soul individually and, once we have cured our own spiritual depression, helping others do the same. Working as a team, and believing in a better, brighter future for the human race, we can make enlightenment a reality. Now wouldn't that be nice.

The First Wave of Awakeners

Five percent of the World's population will have commenced their awakening journey by 2027. This mass event will be largely concentrated in the West. Those who have been selected to awaken are more highly evolved souls, who have typically concluded at least seventy percent of their soul lessons (although there will be exceptions to this rule.) However, not all higher evolved souls will awaken in this lifetime, they may have a different purpose. For example, they may be on the "opposing team" (don't hold it against them, they are just carrying out the mission they've been given) or they may be a "keeper". A keeper is someone whose purpose it is to support another soul through their spiritual awakening on Earth, often a romantic partner. They provide security, financial and otherwise, during what can often be a turbulent time. In their next life they may well be the one to awaken and someone else will act as *their* keeper.

The Seven Major Signs of Spiritual Awakening

If you've begun your conscious awakening, then you're one of the five percent. If you're not sure, then the seven major signs of spiritual awakening are:

1. Developing an intense interest in spiritual matters, including metaphysics and quantum mechanics;

2. Entering a period of enforced downtime, through life events such as redundancy, retirement, bereavement, or chronic illness, or global events like the Covid pandemic;
3. Going through a protracted phase of chronic tiredness and requiring a lot of sleep;
4. Commencing or completing deep inner work, unravelling historical trauma and self-limiting beliefs and behaviors;
5. Starting to have "other-worldly" experiences, such as visions, hearing voices, or receiving premonitions;
6. Making new friends who are on the same spiritual journey as yourself;
7. Becoming aware of synchronicities in your environment, such as recurring number sequences, or butterfly, dragonfly, or bird symbols (these are the most commonly used signs during awakening).

A Definition of "Spiritual Awakening"

Because we're so early in our understanding of ourselves as souls here on Earth, there's no concrete definition of "spiritual awakening" in the human lexicon. I would like to offer one. This definition is based on my experience over the past few years and extensive discussion with my higher self and guides. We think of spiritual awakening as an ephemeral, ineffable experience, but that's not the case. It's easy to understand if we embrace the idea that we're perpetual souls incarnated in physical form, in just one dimension of a multi-dimensional universe. In fact, only a fragment of our total soul is incarnated in our human bodies; part remains in the higher dimensions, other parts are living simultaneous human lives (yes, there is more than one of "you").

Our higher self, or "oversoul" also remains in the higher dimensions. This is the soul we were 'birthed' from when our own soul originally came into being. (Here on Earth we prefer the term "higher self," Sophia calls it the "oversoul." I use these terms interchangeably throughout this book.) This entity is the highest expression of our own soul, replete with universal knowledge and power. We share "soul DNA" with this being and inherit many of its characteristics.

Spiritual awakening, therefore, is the process whereby the earthbound part of ourselves (our soul) reintegrates with our oversoul. Along the way, we dilute our attachment to the physical parts of our system, the body and Ego. As human beings, once we've completed this integration and learned to use the channel connecting us to our oversoul we have created (this final stage of spiritual awakening is known as "transcendence") we have fully awakened and attained a state of enlightenment. This reintegration is both the ultimate goal of spiritual awakening and its definition.

The Four Parts of the Human "Avatar"

In our human form, we think of ourselves as an "I," and as existing purely on the earthly plane, but this is not so. We are a "we." The human system comprises four parts—the body, the soul, the higher self, and the Ego. Taken as a whole, this collaboration is known as an "avatar." The four parts of the human avatar relate to aspects of the mind:

- The subconscious mind represents the body—the seat of automatic response;
- The conscious mind represents the soul—the seat of rational thought;
- The superconscious mind represents the higher self—the seat of intuition; and
- The unconscious mind represents the Ego and is the collection of beliefs we continually generate about ourselves from the moment we are born.

When we talk about "shedding the Ego" as part of spiritual awakening, we are talking about losing beliefs that limit us. Sophia refers to it as "subsuming the Ego." This happens as part of the spiritual awakening process and is fundamental to its success.

Understanding that we're multi-dimensional beings, housed in a human avatar comprised of these four discrete parts, is fundamental to comprehending the spiritual awakening process. Releasing the attachment to thinking of ourselves as an "I" helps us progress in our spiritual journeys.

Chapter 2—How the Dark Night of the Soul Relates to Chakra Health

The root cause of spiritual depression—a Dark Night of the Soul—is poor chakra health. There are two types of Dark Night which I will explain in detail in Chapter 3, and each of these is caused by blockage or constriction of the chakras. Why haven't you heard about this before? Because nobody made the connection. This is just starting to be uncovered now, as part of the mass spiritual awakening. Let's look at the traditional interpretation of the Dark Night before we dive into the importance of the chakras.

The Dark Night of the Soul in Religious Tradition

Until now, the Dark Night of the Soul was understood predominantly in a religious context. The term was given to us by the sixteenth century poem of the same name written by St John of the Cross. There are few documented cases, the other most notable accounts come from St Teresa de Avila, a sixteenth century Spanish nun, and Mother Teresa. For this reason the Dark Night tends to be associated with Christianity, however you do not need to be religious to go through this stage of the spiritual awakening process.

At this time of human history, we also use the term in a loose way to describe:

- a period of torpor or depression;
- a spiritual crisis;

- a hard and painful period in one's life;
- a difficult transition to a deeper, more meaningful way of living.

Why don't we have a fixed, common definition of this kind of spiritual depression today? Largely because we are only at the beginning of the global spiritual awakening and so have few data.

Until recently, only a few people entered the Dark Night of the Soul as a stage of the spiritual awakening journey. Those who did were highly evolved souls on a religious path—religion historically being the route a "spiritual" person would take. This is the reason there are only a tiny number of first-hand accounts of the Dark Night in existence, all of them with Christian roots. Because of the types of people who went through this experience, to the general population, the Dark Night must have felt like something that only happened to the deeply religious.

Therefore, looking back into history, the Dark Night can appear strictly related to a religious journey but in fact, it's a clear-cut, diagnosable condition that can happen at various stages in life, regardless of religious belief, and whether or not we're on a conscious spiritual journey. It's possible you have experienced a Dark Night of the Soul but understood it as something else—a period of depression, or the "blues."

Chakric Constriction and The Dark Night of the Soul

Now let's talk about the Dark Night of the Soul in relation to the chakras. What's going on exactly? It's this. A Dark Night is the mental, emotional, and physical state that occurs when the flow of energy through one or more of the seven main chakras in the human system is reduced to a substantial degree. As I mentioned, there are two types of Dark Night which I'll explore in detail in the next chapter, but here is a brief summary for context: The first type—the *growth-*

oriented Dark Night—can happen at any time although it usually occurs prior to our conscious spiritual awakening. It's caused by our own actions or inactions and/or negative situations. The second type—the *spiritual* Dark Night—commences once our soul is fifty percent integrated with its higher self. It's hard-wired into the spiritual awakening process and is unavoidable, if you're on the journey. Each type of Dark Night of the Soul is caused by a limiting of energy flow through the chakras but it occurs for different reasons and manifests in different ways.

The Function of the Chakras

The chakras are our energy centers and means of connection to the wider universe. My team describes them as "superconductors." A superconductor allows electricity to flow without resistance. Substitute "energy" for "electricity" and you get the idea. The human system cannot operate without some connection to the wider universe. However, it can function on a basic level at as little as five percent of its chakric capacity. The more the energy flow through the chakras constricts, the more severe the symptoms of the Dark Night become.

I appreciate that some readers may have difficulty accepting this idea, especially in the West. However, in Eastern traditions, such as Hinduism and Buddhism, and in holistic medicinal practices such as Ayurvedic Medicine and Traditional Chinese Medicine (TCM), practitioners understand chakras as fundamental to diagnostics and healing. But modern Western medicine does not recognize their existence (despite the efforts of alternative practitioners).

As far back as the Ancient Greeks, philosophers like Plato and Pythagoras gave detailed descriptions of the chakras, as well as the multi-dimensional soul and how it relates to the compartments of the mind. This is the same information my team shared with me and that I outlined in the previous chapter. The West has discarded this knowledge, investing instead in the discipline of "rational" science, which came to prominence in the eighteenth and nineteenth centuries. The reliance on experimentation with replicable results means that most Western scientists now only believe what they can "see."

The Start of the "New Science"

This dogged adherence to materialist science is one reason the work of people such as Russell Targ, the American physicist who led the U.S. government's investigation into remote viewing and other psychic phenomena in the 1970s, is so important. Targ provided compelling evidence that forces we cannot see connect us as a whole[i]. Other brave thinkers, such as psychologist Gary E. Schwartz, are also bucking the norm and conducting similar experiments to Targ, into mediumship and other "paranormal" activities, with outstanding results[ii]. This is the start of the "New Science." If you're interested in this area, I also suggest reading Bruce Lipton and Gregg Braden who are on the leading edge of this thinking.

One day the scientific community will accept that the human system works on multiple levels, not all of which we can perceive, and that universal forces exist beyond those described by conventional science. The New Science will develop over the next two hundred years and will establish chakras as a fundamental system required to sustain human life. Not only that, we will understand spiritual awakening as a specific, physical, metaphysical, and scientific process, which reconnects us as "individuals" to the universal consciousness. That means that the Dark Night of the Soul will become a recognized stage of life, somewhat like adolescence or menopause—a rite of passage, if you like. But we're not there yet and there's little information in the world to go on (hence why I'm writing this book).

If you can accept the fundamental truth that you're a multi-dimensional being connected to the universe via your chakras, congratulations, you're already a pioneer.

A Description of Each of the Seven Chakras

Let's remind ourselves of the seven chakras and their functions. I should add here that this is a simplified description of a complex system. If you're interested in learning more about the "energetic being" I recommend reading Donna Eden or Caroline Myss. So, on a basic level, our chakras live in the "energy body"—a layer of the human system that (most) people can't see, and, as I mentioned, they are our main points of connection to the seven universal energy sources (superconductors). The purer and less interrupted this energy flow is, the better you feel and the more things will go your way. However, sluggish energy flow in any of the chakras can cause negative physical, mental, and emotional symptoms, as well as a downturn in "luck"—all hallmarks of a Dark Night of the Soul.

Below are the seven main chakras and their locations:

- Root—at the base of the spine between the anus and the genitals;
- Sacral—in the lower belly, between the genitals and the navel;
- Solar Plexus—in the upper belly, above the navel;
- Heart—in the center of the chest;
- Throat—in the center of the neck;
- Third Eye—just above the eyebrows, in the middle of the forehead;
- Crown—at the top of the head.

Each chakra corresponds to a color of the rainbow:

- Root = red;
- Sacral = orange;

- Solar Plexus = yellow;
- Heart = green;
- Throat = blue;
- Third Eye = indigo
- Crown = violet (or white).

This energetic rainbow reflects the fact that our entire universe and everything in it, including us, is made of light. It's holographic.

When we're born, our chakras are open and unsullied, which is why children so often display "paranormal" abilities—their free-flowing energy centers bond them to the spiritual realm. As we grow up and conform to the demands of our families, society, and culture, or experience difficult life events, our chakras start to become blocked.

One helpful way to think of the chakras is as a prism. If we open each chakra wide (as in Kundalini yoga), thereby allowing a clear stream of rainbow colors from the cosmos into our bodies, the combined colors create bright white light. This rarest of aura colors represents the highest possible level of spirituality and therefore power. This is the state you're aiming for via your spiritual awakening.

Chakra Blockages Can Also Impact Life Events

I mentioned earlier that, as well as causing negative physical, mental, and emotional symptoms, blocked chakras can cause "bad luck." Why? Much of what happens to you on the physical plane is the product of your own (and others') minds. We're all manifesting our personal and shared reality, day after day. Apart from events instigated by our team on the other side, we're creating our lives as we go. If we're experiencing uncomfortable physical or emotional sensations, and aren't managing them with awareness, this has an enormous effect on our state of mind. We think negatively. Negative thinking begets negative events because we create our own existence with our thoughts. This is an illustration of the fundamental connection between our physical, mental, and external realities.

We all know people who can't seem to catch a break. They are almost certainly experiencing a chronic growth-oriented Dark Night of the Soul. The longer it goes on for, the harder it is to get out of, which is why maintaining chakra health is so important. The protocols in this book help keep your chakras in good condition as well as giving you the tools to repair any damage. With a little effort and focus, and by using the protocols I teach in this book, anyone can reverse a downward trend.

Each chakra governs an area of the human system and is associated with specific behaviors and life events. If you can release the (predominantly Western) attachment to believing that our "physical" beings and our lives are disparate and disconnected, it will help you understand how the chakras work. It's not the case that these things are disconnected, the opposite is true. *Everything* is connected. Once you accept this idea, you'll be able to spot patterns in your reality, linked to chakra function.

Below, I summarize the most common issues for each of the chakras:

Root Chakra

- Physical symptoms: constipation, bladder infections, colon problems, issues with the lower back or skeletal system;
- Emotional and mental symptoms: anxiety, sluggishness, eating disorders, obsessive compulsive disorder, unstable mood, living in fear, phobia;
- Real-world symptoms: money worries, loss of stability (for example, losing a job or a home), family problems, being attacked or bullied.

Sacral Chakra

- Physical symptoms: reproductive issues, disorders of the womb and genitals, STDs, loss of libido, pre- and post-menstrual complications, spleen and kidney problems;
- Emotional and mental symptoms: sexual compulsions or disorders, perversion, co-dependency;
- Real-world symptoms: relationship problems, destructive partnerships.

Solar Plexus Chakra

- Physical symptoms: digestive issues, loss of appetite, over-eating, diabetes, food allergies, chronic fatigue;
- Emotional and mental symptoms: addiction, loss of motivation, low self-esteem, depression, weak-will, lack of energy, creative blocks, mental fog, aggressive behavior;
- Real-world symptoms: attracting people who mistreat you, losing things that were once important to you, ending of friendships, diminished social life, poor results at work.

Heart Chakra

- Physical symptoms: diminished immune system, problems with the heart and lungs, poor circulation, high or low blood pressure, respiratory problems;
- Emotional and mental symptoms: lack of empathy, over-feeling, depression, struggling to forgive, selfishness, an inability to "let go," jealousy, spiteful behavior;
- Real-world symptoms: relationship issues, attracting narcissists or those with predatory behaviors, falling out with people, arguments.

Throat Chakra

- Physical symptoms: neck pain, thyroid issues, recurring sore throat, loss of voice, mouth ulcers, dental problems;
- Emotional and mental symptoms: social anxiety, shyness, lying behaviors, struggling to express thoughts, loss of identity, introversion, avoidance of tough conversations, feeling you have "lost" yourself, depression, confused thoughts, escapism;
- Real-world symptoms: the breakdown of communication in personal and professional spheres, being lied to, damaging relationships with lying or incommunicative behavior, the distancing of friendships, loss of creative outlets or deterioration in creative output.

Third Eye Chakra

- Physical symptoms: headaches and migraines, eye problems, brain disorders, insomnia, imbalance of the endocrine system;
- Emotional and mental symptoms: paranoia, hallucinations, difficulty concentrating, nightmares, obsession with the occult or paranormal, inability to focus, loss of intuition, a decrease in imagination, loss of the ability to visualize, feeling a lack of connection;
- Real-world symptoms: negative events arising as the result of poor decision-making, isolation caused by avoiding others, problems at work due to lack of focus, being committed to a mental institution, bad luck arising from negative manifestation.

Crown Chakra

- Physical symptoms: brain disorders, chronic fatigue, headaches and migraines, hair loss, amnesia, pituitary gland issues, sensitivity to light and sound;
- Emotional and mental symptoms: a need for isolation, feeling cut off, existential angst, self-doubt, psychosis, loss of self-belief, confusion, mistrust, paranoia, suicidal depression;
- Real-world symptoms: loss of religious or spiritual beliefs, withdrawal from life, rash decisions leading to negative outcomes, deterioration of relationships.

As you can see, having a chakra blockage isn't fun. But take heart: by introducing beneficial behaviors to your life, you can clear them with just a little focus and open up new and exciting possibilities. Not to mention drawing ever closer to a state of personal enlightenment.

Chapter 3—The Two Types of the Dark Night of the Soul

As we now know, the Dark Night of the Soul occurs when the energy flow through our chakras is constricted—but why do these constrictions happen in the first place? Let's first remind ourselves briefly of the two types of Dark Night of the Soul:

- The first, which can occur at any time in your life, but is often found in the early stages of unconscious spiritual awakening, before we are even aware we *are* awakening, is growth-oriented. That means it's designed to stimulate you to make positive improvements to yourself or your life;

- The second is a specific stage in the spiritual awakening journey and is hardwired into the awakening process. All of your chakras are automatically constricted once your soul reaches fifty percent integration with your higher self (you can reach this milestone without being fully conscious that you're going through a spiritual awakening).

Let's look at each type of the Dark Night of the Soul in detail, starting with the growth-oriented Dark Night.

The Growth-Oriented Dark Night of the Soul

We all know what we're supposed to do, but we don't always do it:

- eat a healthy diet;
- avoid alcohol and drugs;
- get eight hours' sleep;
- meditate;
- exercise;
- spend time in nature;
- show kindness to ourselves and others;
- live in an honest, ethical way;
- invest in our self-development;
- remove ourselves from situations that make us unhappy.

If we don't pay attention to our well-being and behaviors, we will experience chakra issues. This includes blockages caused by another's actions or an unhappy situation, such as a broken relationship or a job we hate. It's up to us to extricate ourselves and to *grow*. In the case of depression brought about by damaging or traumatic events, such as bereavement or divorce, then we must equip ourselves with the tools to navigate through. This, again, is growth.

Very few people have chakras in perfect health. In fact, it's normal to have some degree of blockage in our cosmic superconductors. Serious problems arise when one or more is constricted to fifty percent or less of capacity. This is the point at which we find ourselves in a growth-oriented Dark Night of the Soul. Will you enter a spiritual depression if you eat fast food twice a week or get cross with your partner from time to time? Probably not. Will you enter it if you abuse substances, mistreat people, or tolerate situations you know are bad for you? It's possible, even likely.

The good news is that we don't have to behave "perfectly" to enjoy reasonable chakra health and open ourselves to the potential it presents. Sophia and the other members of my team advocate the 80/20 rule. Follow a healthy "spiritual" lifestyle eighty percent of the time, but cut yourself a little slack with the other twenty percent.

Where things go wrong is when we're operating at 50/50 or 20/80, or are allowing an unpleasant situation to become desperate.

The Impact of Childhood Experiences on Chakra Health

Sometimes we inherit poor chakra health from our childhoods. For example, if we undergo great trauma or we aren't taught to live in a healthy and ethical way, our chakras will become blocked from an early age. In addition, we're unlikely to have been shown the tools we need to extricate ourselves. But with focus and determination in adulthood, we can do it. And we should always remember that we plan our childhoods before we incarnate, so whatever occurs (strange as it may seem) is what we need to learn our soul lessons. Indeed, the tougher the circumstances, the more we learn. The universe never gives us a problem we can't solve (not to say that the solving will be easy).

Not All Chakras are Blocked During a Growth-Oriented Dark Night

One of the defining features of a growth-oriented Dark Night of the Soul is that typically only one or a few of the chakras are constricted to fifty percent or less of capacity. This means it can take hold in a low level way—a "slump." It's one reason it's harder to identify than a spiritual Dark Night of the Soul—are you just going through a bad patch? Tomayto, tomahto. We can almost always track physical, mental, and emotional problems, coupled with negative events happening in our lives, back to chakra issues. We could say that the growth-oriented Dark Night happens along a spectrum. People experience it in different ways depending on which chakras are blocked and to what degree. For a few, it can deteriorate into crisis or a breakdown.

A Growth-Oriented Dark Night Can Lead to Conscious Awakening

The good news about a growth-oriented Dark Night of the Soul, however mild or severe, is that it can be a springboard into the conscious spiritual awakening journey. As souls, we are indomitable. In each of us is a tough center, capable of transforming the life we have chosen to live in this incarnation. The universe would never leave us in a situation we can't repair, and that's the truth. Many people going through tough times find their way to spirituality in one of its many guises:

- religion;
- Buddhism;
- meditation;
- holistic treatments;
- metaphysics;
- the paranormal;
- clean living;
- therapy;
- deep inner work;
- creating art.

Each of these areas is a potential route to enlightenment—understanding ourselves as immortal souls who choose to experience life as human beings through multiple incarnations. For many people, the need to restore chakra health—consciously or unconsciously—is the impetus they require to explore these kinds of topics. These newly acquired interests and behaviors can become a springboard for conscious awakening. Indeed, our teams will often try to use them as such.

The Symptoms of the Growth-Oriented Dark Night of the Soul

A growth-oriented Dark Night can arrive suddenly due to a traumatic event or, more typically, manifest as a slow decline. This is because our chakras are becoming gradually more blocked as we continue with damaging situations or behaviors. As I said earlier, we can think of the growth-oriented Dark Night as occurring along a spectrum. We move back and forth depending on how we're managing ourselves and our lives.

There's an enormous breadth of potential symptoms associated with the growth-oriented Dark Night of the Soul which, again, depend on which chakras are blocked and to what degree. In fact, you have almost certainly experienced a growth-oriented Dark Night at least once in your life but not understood it as such. As an illustration, which of the following examples do you think are associated with a growth-oriented Dark Night of the Soul?

- suffering from General Anxiety Disorder (GAD);
- chronic stomach pain;
- persistent headaches;
- burning out at work;
- losing a large sum of money.

The answer, of course, is all of them. Negative states of mind, physical infirmities, and many unhappy life events, have their root cause in chakra blockage.

Having said this, there are some common symptoms to a growth-oriented Dark Night of the Soul. Whichever chakra(s) is blocked, you are likely to experience one or more of these to a greater or lesser degree:

- low mood;
- a feeling that everything is pointless;
- loss of interest in things you once loved;
- difficulty "getting going;"
- feeling you have "lost" yourself;
- existential angst ("what's it all for?");
- looking for solace in alcohol or drugs;
- niggling minor illnesses that may escalate into something more serious over time;
- being unable to "catch a break;"
- life stalling or going backward.

The person most able to diagnose a growth-oriented Dark Night of the Soul is the one going through it. Ask yourself these questions:

- "Do I feel like myself?"
- "Am I happy?"
- "Does my life hold meaning?"
- "Does something fundamental need to change?"

The answers to these questions will help you assess if you're going through a growth-oriented spiritual depression.

How Long Does the Growth-Oriented Dark Night of the Soul Last?

Unlike the spiritual Dark Night of the Soul, the growth-oriented Dark Night is open-ended. In other words, it will persist until you make the necessary changes to your behavior or life and so experience growth. As I said, you can always climb out of a growth-oriented Dark Night, no matter how deep or chronic. How long it takes corresponds to the amount of chakra repair you need.

The Purpose of the Growth-Oriented Dark Night of the Soul

The purpose of a growth-oriented Dark Night is to stimulate change. Our deepening unhappiness alerts us to the fact that all is not well in our world. It's the universe's way of telling us to take a different path. The change needed can be in behavior or circumstance, but it's always change for the better. The negative effects we experience from prolonged or severe chakra constriction serve as a tool to steer us towards a more beneficial path. As I mentioned earlier, a growth-oriented Dark Night can also be a springboard into a more spiritual way of life and a precursor to conscious awakening. It often prompts deep inner work, which is needed to build a stable foundation to support the conscious spiritual awakening journey.

The Spiritual Dark Night of the Soul

This Dark Night of the Soul is the highly recognizable type which takes place around the middle of the spiritual awakening process. It's easy to spot because, unlike during a growth-oriented Dark Night, all the chakras are constricted at the same time, to the same degree. This means everyone experiences similar symptoms. The severity of the spiritual Dark Night of the Soul varies from person to person, depending on how much they need to learn from the experience and the nature of their mission. However, everyone who goes through this type of spiritual depression will have a strong sense of being "disconnected" from the universe.

The spiritual Dark Night starts automatically when the soul reaches fifty percent integration with the higher self. If we follow the requisite protocols, we exit the spiritual Dark Night of the Soul at between sixty-five and seventy percent integration. If we don't, we slip backwards and "de-integrate", until we exit the spiritual Dark Night the way we came in. As soon as we reach fifty percent integration once more, the whole process starts again.

The Stage Prior to the Spiritual Dark Night of the Soul

The stage of awakening prior to the spiritual Dark Night is one of connection. We feel deeply enmeshed with the universe, our higher self, and guides, and typically develop one or more of the "clairs":

- clairaudience—the ability to hear communication from the "other side;"
- clairvoyance—the ability to see spirit visitors from the other side ;
- clairsentience—the ability to feel others' emotions;
- claircognizance—the ability to "just know" things;
- clairalience (the ability to smell things that are not present on the physical plane), and
- clairgustance (the ability to taste things that are not present on the physical plane).

We may also find we've developed telepathic abilities and powers of premonition.

The Spiritual Dark Night of the Soul Arrives Suddenly

A striking feature of the spiritual Dark Night of the Soul is that it descends almost overnight. Within twenty-four hours we go from being deeply connected to feeling totally isolated. This sharp transition from connection to disconnection makes it easy to spot this kind of Dark Night. Typically there's a short lead up to it where things feel "off" —communication buzzes in and out or becomes distorted— but by and large, it's as though a switch has been flicked.

In my own case, where I had become used to the constant companionship of Sophia, Om, and Freya, suddenly, I had *silence*. Not only that, where I had been enjoying the experience of being "in flow" and my manifestation powers had seemed limitless, this reversed. Not only did things start going wrong, I couldn't do anything about it. I was grief-stricken. I felt abandoned, alone, and cut off from the universal consciousness that sustains every one of us.

Our Teams Dislike the Dark Night of the Soul Too

Once I'd worked my way through the spiritual Dark Night of the Soul (on my second attempt) and was back in communication with my guides, I learned that our teams don't like the Dark Night any more than we do. Think about it. These beings have invested considerable time and energy into helping us find the path we chose for ourselves before we incarnated into this life. They are our buddies, our "team"— they're rooting for us. More than that, they love us. So, do they like it when they can't help us? Of course not! Keeping this in mind when I went through the Dark Night for the second time was a great motivator. I wasn't just doing it for myself, I was doing it for my team too.

As I said earlier, the spiritual Dark Night of the Soul is a fundamental stage in the awakening journey. It will happen to all of us who progress to a certain stage of awakening and there's nothing we can do to prevent it. All we can do is trust the process, follow the protocols, and have faith that something magnificent—the opportunity to reclaim our birth right as souls—lies on the other side.

The Symptoms of the Spiritual Dark Night of the Soul

The most obvious symptom of the spiritual Dark Night of the Soul is the flicking of the switch from connected to disconnected. Beyond this, it usually manifests in a similar way in everyone, although, as I mentioned, some will feel it more keenly than others. In the most severe cases, the energy flow through the chakras is reduced to five percent, the minimum required to sustain human life.

The wider symptoms of the spiritual Dark Night of the Soul manifest in two different ways. The first is born of the sudden absence of communication. This can give rise to:

- a sense of loss;
- feelings of abandonment;
- anger;
- frustration;
- loneliness;
- grief;
- self-doubt.

The second is the direct result of all of our chakras being constricted simultaneously. We enter a sort of depression, but it's different to a "normal" depression because we can't feel much at all. Instead of the customary sadness, we have a pervasive sense of clench-jawed grimness (this is the best way I can find to describe it). We feel "lobotomised", as though a vital part of our being has been cut away (which indeed it has). Other associated symptoms are:

- lack of motivation;
- lethargy;
- apathy;
- withdrawal from society;
- abandonment of previous beneficial behaviors.

Fatigue is a Common Physical Symptom of the Spiritual Dark Night of the Soul

There is also a physical symptom that typifies the spiritual Dark Night of the Soul and that's fatigue. I'm talking about a bone-deep tiredness similar to Chronic Fatigue Syndrome (in fact, this can happen at various stages of the spiritual awakening journey, but is almost always present during the Dark Night). This means you need to sleep more than usual, perhaps for long periods during the day. Your team will facilitate this by causing you to fall ill, or arranging matters so you can take time away from work. While this can feel stressful, remember, your team has your back and will make sure you have money to support yourself.

So, why the lack of energy and need for sleep? There are three main reasons:

1. Time to Process

The first is "processing" time. During your spiritual awakening—and especially leading up to the spiritual Dark Night of the Soul—you will learn an enormous amount about yourself and how the universe works. You need to absorb and "process" this information, which is done most easily while you're asleep. In fact, during this time, you may find yourself dreaming more, with greater vividness, as your mind works through this new information.

2. Time to Heal

You need "healing" time. Spiritual awakening, even undertaken slowly, is intense, and your mental, emotional, and physical systems come under strain. It's a uniquely demanding experience. Fortunately, the work you did leading up to the spiritual Dark Night means your system is strong—otherwise, you would not have come this far. Still, it's important to respect the process and understand you are undergoing a form of "rebirth."

3. *You're Being Upgraded*

Your team is mending and "upgrading" your system while you're sleeping. This is to strengthen your mind and body so you can progress to the next stage of awakening and onward to enlightenment.

The Spiritual Dark Night of the Soul Rarely Causes Serious Illness or "Bad Luck"

The good news about the spiritual Dark Night of the Soul is that, unlike the growth-oriented Dark Night, you're unlikely to experience major illness or a significant shift in your circumstances. It seems we're insulated from these effects of chakra blockage during this period. You may experience "niggly" things but nothing serious. This is excepting any (pseudo-)illness your team has instigated to ensure you get rest during the spiritual Dark Night. In this case, they have full control and the condition will mysteriously disappear at the appropriate time. Any real harm that befalls us during the spiritual Dark Night tends to arise from our own behaviors. That's because during this time we're more likely to:

- seek solace in drink and drugs;
- abandon our spiritual practice;
- eat poorly or not at all;
- stop exercising;
- withdraw from family and friends; and
- think negatively.

All of these things will affect us in uncomfortable ways and, more significantly, prevent us from getting through the spiritual Dark Night of the Soul to the other side. The irony of the situation is that, at exactly the time you need to double-down on your good behaviors, it's the last thing you want to do. That's why the spiritual Dark Night is difficult to get through, unless you have a daily routine you can focus on and stick to.

How Long Does the Spiritual Dark Night of the Soul Last?

On your first attempt at getting through the spiritual Dark Night, Sophia tells me that three months is typically the shortest amount of time it can take. This assumes you're following the protocols consistently. (Whilst my team normally advocates the 80/20 rule, during the spiritual Dark Night they encourage 100/0, to help you get through as quickly as possible.) If you follow some, but not all of the protocols, or follow them, but erratically, then this time period will stretch out. However, it's unlikely to last more than nine months.

If you abandon all healthy, spiritual behaviors from the get-go, then you should exit in no longer than two months, sliding backwards along the spiritual awakening continuum. However, in this instance, you will just re-enter the spiritual Dark Night of the Soul the next time you reach fifty percent integration with your higher self, so it's much better to grit your teeth and focus on pushing through, unless you intend to abandon your awakening journey all together (please don't, we need you).

When you're in the spiritual Dark Night of the Soul, three to nine months seems like a lifetime and almost impossible to endure. I promise you, once you're out the other side, it quickly fades into a dim distant memory. No part of the spiritual awakening journey will ever be as tough again, if you keep moving forward.

Going Through the Spiritual Dark Night More Than Once

If you fail to get through the spiritual Dark Night of the Soul on the first time of asking, you will find your second attempt is much easier. It's also much shorter. It seems we retain some kind of "muscle memory" or foundation we can build on top of. For myself, the first experience of the spiritual Dark Night of the Soul lasted nearly four months (I slid backwards), the second just three weeks (I got through it). So however hard it seems, just keep going. The light at the end of the tunnel may be just around the corner.

Reaching the End of the Spiritual Dark Night of the Soul

You'll know when you've reached the end of the spiritual Dark Night of the Soul. All of a sudden, communication crackles back into life, like a longwave radio tuning into a station. You will find your low mood lifts more or less overnight. This type of spiritual depression departs as quickly as it arrives. Connection and joy quickly return. Note that, during the spiritual Dark Night of the Soul you still get some messages from your guides. They are few and far between and feel very distant, but they do arrive occasionally. The more you adhere to the protocols, the easier it is for them to communicate with you.

The Purpose of the Spiritual Dark Night of the Soul

The spiritual Dark Night of the Soul has several functions, the majority of which are to teach us lessons. It might not feel like at it the time, but we're learning a lot during this stage of spiritual awakening.

Lesson 1: Resilience

The first, critical, lesson is resilience. Highly evolved souls often need to work on this as part of their awakening journey. Typically we have experienced trauma, usually in our early lives. As noted previously, this is intentional and in line with the plan we made before we incarnated. We embark on a challenging life for three main reasons. First, because it anchors us to the physical plane, otherwise our minds would go whizzing off into the stratosphere at the earliest opportunity and it would be difficult for our teams to manage the timing of our awakening. Second, so we can develop empathy with others who have undergone great pain and, third, so we can learn how to extricate ourselves from the mental chains such experiences create. This, in turn, means we can teach and help others.

We process most of our personal trauma before we reach the spiritual Dark Night of the Soul—we have to, otherwise we wouldn't progress so far—but typically we need to build ourselves up a little more. This is normal and part of the process. Most significantly, these types of mental limits reduce our resilience—our ability to cope with the things life throws at us. Those of us awakening at this time have important missions. We need to be strong to deliver them. Discovering that we can survive the Dark Night of the Soul is the proof we need that we can get through anything.

In my case, I exited the spiritual Dark Night of the Soul a stronger, more capable person who refused to allow herself to be fazed by anything. This is in stark contrast to the person I was before I started my spiritual awakening and just one more thing I am grateful that this process has given me.

Lesson 2: Self-Sufficiency and Autonomy

Going through the Dark Night of the Soul also teaches us "self-sufficiency" and "autonomy." The Oxford English Dictionary defines autonomy as: "Free will; self-governing, ability of a person or a group to choose a course of action." The danger with the glorious, heady period of connection leading up to the spiritual Dark Night of the Soul is that we give up our free will. Instead, we look to our guides to tell us, "What should I do?" This is entirely contrary to the purpose of incarnation on Earth. We are supposed to make our own decisions (and mistakes) so we can learn.

One of the most significant things I've learned during my spiritual awakening is that it's up to *us* to decide what we want. Then our team will help us get there. Sure, if we want something that isn't right for us, they may not make the path easy, hoping we'll change our mind, but it's our choice how we want to live our lives, including making the decision to do things we know aren't right or good for us.

You Are the CEO of Your Own Life

In the early stages of my awakening my team told me: "You are the CEO of your own life." This was news to me. Once I understood that I *had* a team, I started to view myself as its instrument. I thought I was here to do whatever was required of me, a servant to a bigger cause. I revered my guides as "higher beings" and was later surprised to find this is something they neither enjoy nor want. Rather, they consider themselves our lieutenants, smoothing the way for us and carrying out our instructions. It took me a long time to understand this but once the concept finally bedded in, I felt empowered and unstoppable, capable of achieving anything, with the backing of my extraordinary team.

The lack of communication during the Dark Night of the Soul forces us to depend once more on our own resources. We have no way of reaching our guides, we're the only person who can decide what route to take. At this time it's also typical for our usual methods of seeking advice to stop working—sign-reading and tarot card divination, for example. We become our own person once again. This rediscovered autonomy "trains" us back into a self-sufficient way of thinking which persists beyond the Dark Night.

Lesson 3: Adopting a Regular Spiritual Routine

The third purpose of the spiritual Dark Night of the Soul is to push us to establish a regular spiritual routine. It's vital during this stage of awakening to continue integrating with our higher selves (remember, we exit the spiritual Dark Night at around sixty five to seventy percent integration). Refining and cementing our daily protocols during this time is essential to overcoming the Dark Night, even though we can't feel them "working". This forced adherence to ritual creates beneficial habits which stand us in good stead once we're on the other side. Without dogged adherence to spiritual practices (which encompass things you might not have realized—all included in this book), you will not make it through the spiritual Dark Night of the Soul.

The Spiritual Dark Night is Also an Assessment Tool

There's a final reason the spiritual Dark Night of the Soul is so important, which is not a lesson as such. How you respond to it lets you and your team identify if you're ready to progress to the next stage of awakening. If you're struggling with resilience, autonomy, or resisting learning new techniques, you're not ready. It's only when you gain mastery of mind, and demonstrate the strength and commitment needed to overcome the spiritual Dark Night, that you're capable of progression.

Can't we just avoid the Spiritual Dark Night of the Soul altogether?

It's natural to ask ourselves "why not remain in the blissful stage just before the Dark Night of the Soul and not go through it at all?" Unfortunately, this isn't an option, for several reasons.

Reason One

The first reason is the valuable lessons and techniques that the Dark Night teaches us, as outlined in the previous section. These are essential to our development as spiritual beings incarnated in a human body on Earth. Prior to the Dark Night we've learned very little, even though we may believe we have this thing all worked out. We don't. In fact, from my own experience, even after completing the final stage of awakening—transcendence—we still have more to learn. Remaining in the comfortable zone prior to the Dark Night might be enjoyable but it would do little to advance us spiritually.

Reason Two

The second reason is that, even if we wanted to avoid the Dark Night, it's nigh on impossible. The only way to do so would be to abandon our spiritual development entirely and resume a state of non-awareness. This *is* possible—we can ask our teams to halt the awakening process. However, the reason we've been chosen to be in this first wave of awakeners is because we almost certainly won't do that! So assuming we keep going in the journey, we will always hit the border of the Dark Night at fifty percent integration with our higher selves. If we then struggle to get through it, start to "de-integrate," and slip backward, we will just keep finding ourselves butting up against it the next time we reach fifty percent. We would yo-yo in and out of the Dark Night. So really our only options are to either remove ourselves from the awakening process completely, or push on through to the other side.

Reason Three

The third reason we should embrace the Dark Night of the Soul and commit to getting through it, is that what's on the other side is spectacular. It's more than worth a few months of misery, trust me.

Every time we complete another stage of awakening, or learn a new lesson or technique, we grow our power. By the time we reach the end of the process we are truly the CEOs of our own lives. You won't go through anything as difficult as the spiritual Dark Night of the Soul again in the rest of your awakening journey, so you can push through with the knowledge that, after this, everything gets easier.

Identifying Which Type of Dark Night You're In

If you're reading this book, it's likely that you (or a loved one) suspect they're going through a Dark Night of the Soul. The questionnaire below will help you understand which type of Dark Night it is. To recap briefly, the two types of Dark Night of the Soul are:

The Growth-Oriented Dark Night

A growth-oriented Dark Night of the Soul is occasioned by our own actions or inactions, or a damaging situation in our lives. It typically happens prior to our formal spiritual awakening. Symptoms of a growth-oriented Dark Night range from mild to severe and manifest in multifarious ways, although they are always accompanied by a sense of unhappiness. The duration of a growth-oriented Dark Night can be as little as two weeks, or as long as a lifetime.

The Spiritual Dark Night

The spiritual Dark Night of the Soul occurs during the awakening process, between fifty and seventy percent integration of our souls and higher selves. It's characterised by a sharp disconnection from our guides and the universe which takes place abruptly, materialising over twenty-four hours. Typically it will not last longer than nine months, after which we will "reconnect."

Which Type of Dark Night Are You in?—Questionnaire.

Circle answer A or B for each question, or make a note on a piece of paper if you're reading this on an e-reader.

Did your Dark Night of the Soul appear?

- A. Gradually, or
- B. Rather suddenly?

If you have suffered from depressive episodes in the past, does this Dark Night feel:

- A. The same, or
- B. Different?

Have you ever had contact with your guides or higher self?

- A. No
- B. Yes

Do you consider yourself to be a spiritual person?

- A. No
- B. Yes

Do you think you're going through a spiritual awakening?

- A. No
- B. Yes

Prior to this episode of the Dark Night of the Soul, were your energy levels:

A. Normal, or
B. Reduced?

Do you have a strong interest in spiritual matters?

A. No
B. Yes

Are you aware that you have psychic abilities, such as one of the clairs, or the ability to sense future events?

A. No
B. Yes

Do you meditate, or have you meditated in the past?

A. No
B. Yes

Is your emotional state:

A. Erratic up and down, or
B. Damped down and tending toward numbness?

Mostly A's—you're almost certainly experiencing a growth-oriented Dark Night of the Soul.

Mostly B's—you're probably going through a spiritual Dark Night of the Soul.

If you're going through a Dark Night—whichever type—please take heart. It's a temporary situation which is surmountable if you use the protocols in the second half of this book. As the wise Buddhists say, "this too shall pass".

Chapter 4—The Other Side of The Dark Night of the Soul

Whichever type of the Dark Night of the Soul you're experiencing, great things lie in wait on the other side. Let's take a look at the growth-oriented Dark Night of the Soul first.

Reaching The Other Side of the Growth-Oriented Dark Night of the Soul

To get through a growth-oriented Dark Night, as you now know, requires making positive changes to your behavior and circumstances. If you make these changes then, self-evidently, things will improve for you, often radically. You will find yourself in a happier state of mind and a better place. Most significantly, if this change has required you to grow through doing inner work, as it often does, you should be feeling more emotionally calm and stable. This alone has the ability to transform your life.

Also, as I mentioned previously, the work you undertake to get through a growth-oriented Dark Night of the Soul also has the potential to trigger your conscious spiritual awakening. Not only will new beneficial behaviors clear your chakra blockage(s) they will also aid integration with your higher self. As I mentioned, it's common for our teams to use a growth-oriented Dark Night of the Soul as a means to encourage us along the awakening path.

Reaching the Other Side of the Spiritual Dark Night of the Soul

Exiting the spiritual Dark Night of the Soul is not the end of your spiritual awakening journey. However, the subsequent stages are easier and even enjoyable. You have more integration work to do, so sticking to the daily routine you established during your Dark Night is vital, otherwise you may slip backward and find yourself once more on the fringes of spiritual depression.

Besides completing your integration (which should happen within a few months of exiting the spiritual Dark Night of the Soul), the phase after the spiritual Dark Night is one of intense, advanced learning. This period of study and practical application of everything you've learned will propel you rapidly towards a state of enlightenment. It's not uncommon around this time for us to realise we've become a "different person". In fact, what we're doing is rediscovering our true soul nature. This learning phase isn't always easy but brings enormous, beneficial change.

Once we're 100 percent integrated with our higher selves, we move onto the final stage of awakening—transcendence. By the end of transcendence we have utterly transformed ourselves and our lives. Below I list twenty-four benefits and skills you will acquire if you commit to completing the full awakening journey.

1. You Will Learn to Detach

Detachment is the ability to observe events without experiencing extreme emotions and remaining impartial to outcomes. It's a key pillar of Zen Buddhism. If we want to change the world, this skill is crucial. When we feel distress, anger, or another powerful emotion, be it on a political, social, or personal level, it's difficult to be useful. If you're going through a spiritual Dark Night, I assure you, you are a higher evolved soul who came here to be useful. You have a mission, a "higher purpose," and you will struggle to fulfil your purpose if you allow emotion to rule your judgment. Remember, potent emotions, especially negative ones, are generated by the body and subconscious mind, whereas logic comes from the soul and conscious mind. Our goal is to subdue the physical and lead with the rational soul, on our route to integration with our higher selves.

Does Detachment Mean We Stop Caring?

Detachment doesn't mean we stop caring. Our emotions and empathy are still there, but we become the observer rather than the experiencer. It means we're leading with our conscious minds rather than allowing our subconscious minds to take control. We're no longer at the mercy of our autonomic responses. Instead of being buffeted by our emotions, we apply logic and rational thought to any situation.

Detachment Helps Self-Development

When we're detached, we can absorb feedback, criticism, and even insult, without taking it personally. This is an essential skill. If you practice detachment you will come to realise that taking offence is nonsensical. Think of it this way: if someone gives you negative feedback, or attacks you, one of two things is happening. Either you occasioned it (in which case be grateful, for they've opened your eyes to your behavior and given you the opportunity to change), or they themselves have issues that made them attack (in which case feel compassion, for they're carrying an enormous emotional burden).

I was lucky that, during my corporate career, I had to learn to take feedback to survive and progress. (I say "lucky" but of course I and my team had planned that path before I incarnated!) So, I know from experience how deeply uncomfortable criticism can be. None of us likes to have our failings pointed out and few of us enjoy confrontation. However, once I'd mastered the skill of taking people's comments on board, I found I could learn and develop exponentially.

It's a skill I still use today, inviting feedback to help me improve myself and my work.

Detachment Helps Shed the Ego

One outcome of learning to detach is that it helps you "shed your Ego". Recall that this part of you is the amalgamation of beliefs about yourself you started to collect from the moment you were born. Often, these beliefs are self-limiting. We always keep part of our Ego—five percent is the minimum—because that's what makes us uniquely individual. However, shedding other ninety-five percent makes us more empathetic, less defensive, and therefore more effective in the world.

Our Emotions Stabilise

The other benefit of learning detachment is you cease to feel extreme emotions. This is of enormous help if, like me, your natural personality is highly emotional. As you learn to detach, you realize you've stopped riding the emotional rollercoaster. You're in control of your responses, able to remain level-headed and calm in all kinds of situations, and can attain (and maintain) a sense of peace and contentment.

Our Teams Find Creative Ways to Teach Detachment

My team found a novel way to teach me to detach. I have a cat called Minnie, with whom I'm extraordinarily close. I adopted her from a rescue center some years ago and we've become great buddies (she's sitting beside me right now). While I was being taught detachment, Minnie would go missing, sometimes for a couple of days at a time. This was unusual, and caused me a great deal of worry. But once I understood her antics were designed to help me learn to detach, I made a conscious mental effort to set my fears aside. This is called compartmentalization and is a crucial tool of detachment. Lo-and-behold, as I learned to stay calm, she reappeared. It took a few episodes like this for me to master the skill but she always returned (for which I'm grateful—she's my girl). Now I'm able to set aside whatever is occupying my mind or causing me stress and get on with my life and my plans.

2. *You Will Develop Better Judgment*

Your team starts teaching you judgement prior to the Dark Night of the Soul, but they'll accelerate your learning once you're out the other side. How? Typically either by refusing to give you information or giving you false direction. They're pushing you to make your own call. Once you've made a decision, they will then discuss it with you, closing the 'feedback loop'. By analysing our decisions and seeing what we could have done differently, we improve our judgment.

Immediately after I exited the spiritual Dark Night, if I asked my team for direction they would give me increasingly preposterous guidance. I soon learned how to use my internal signals to sense the best course, becoming ever more self-sufficient. This also helped build my confidence.

3. *Your Confidence Will Increase*

Like most higher evolved souls, I experienced a lot of negative events in the first half of my life that caused me to have low self-esteem. Despite having a successful corporate career, I suffered from imposter syndrome (as many women do) and struggled to value myself. It was difficult to shake off the feelings of inadequacy I'd been collecting since childhood. Several years of deep inner work prior to my awakening resolved the majority of my self-esteem and confidence issues, but not all.

Finding my way out of the Dark Night of the Soul contributed significantly to my sense of ability and self-worth. Being pushed to make my own decisions and discovering I could choose positive, self-affirming paths helped me cement my belief in myself. And of course, the ongoing process of shedding the Ego, which is fundamental to spiritual awakening, meant that the last of those old, negative thoughts I had about myself finally evaporated. Now I'm aware of my abilities and limitations, I don't see my failures as reflecting my inadequacy, but as an opportunity to learn.

4. *You Will Gain Proficiency in Spiritual Techniques*

During the spiritual Dark Night of the Soul—and as a requirement of exiting it—you both gain new spiritual techniques and master the ones you're already using. These techniques or "protocols" are more than just a tool to get you through a Dark Night. They're the route to reclaiming your innate skills as a soul while incarnated on the physical plane. In the higher dimensions, we're used to a more elevated state of being. We:

- can manifest whatever we want;
- are comfortable in our "skins;"
- have a clear idea of who we are;
- are aware of our abilities and talents;
- know what we need to improve;
- are compassionate and kind;
- put others before ourselves;
- work together in co-operation for the greater good.

Employing and perfecting spiritual protocols here on Earth allows us to reclaim this state of being. In the higher dimensions, we don't have the trappings of the human system which so often hold us back—the subconscious mind and its big brother, the Ego. While these parts of the human system are trying to help us, they lean toward negativity. They're trying to de-risk our behavior, which means they give rise to self-limiting beliefs and detrimental emotions (such as fear, hate, and greed).

When we become proficient in our spiritual protocols and employ them over time, we subsume the Ego, release ourselves from the autonomic responses of the subconscious, operate with our conscious mind, and reconnect to our higher self, restoring our natural soul state and abilities. So, the more proficient you become in the wider spiritual protocols, the more easily you'll attain this mode. In turn your life on Earth will become more fulfilling, enjoyable, and useful.

5. *You Will Establish a Daily Spiritual Routine*

As well as having new techniques, by the time you exit the spiritual Dark Night of the Soul, you will have established at least the foundations of a regular spiritual routine—hopefully daily. And guess what? You'll love it! With the Dark Night a mere speck in the rear-view mirror, you start to feel the benefits that a solid, consistently practiced, spiritual routine provides, such as deep connection with your team.

It's important to establish a daily practice, even if you don't complete the full ritual every day, as the entire universe works on a twenty-four-hour cycle, the same as on Earth. Each morning you need to refresh and restart, otherwise you'll see the spiritual benefits you're enjoying start to fade. Daily practice keeps you well-connected to your guides, higher self, and universe, with all of the benefits this brings.

6. *You Will Develop a New Type of Relationship With Your Guides*

For myself, one of the most notable features of life beyond the spiritual Dark Night of the Soul was that the foundations of my relationship with my guides and higher self changed. Having grasped the idea that I was the CEO of my own life, I now regarded my team as peers, rather than as all-knowing, all-powerful entities elevated far above me. We're the same as our guides, we're just living in different dimensions. Your team will always be at a similar level of evolution as you, although they may have differing, complementary skills. You are peers in every sense of the word.

I discovered that Sophia, Om, and Freya, all had wonderful senses of humour. Before long, we were chatting like old friends (which of course we are), teasing and pulling each other's legs. Now, even though my work means I spend an enormous amount of time "on my own," I'm never alone. These friends are available at the drop of a hat. Because they know me so well, they always offer the right words at the right times—assuming, of course, that I've kept my connection nice and strong by committing to my daily spiritual routine.

I'm sure you'll establish similar relationships with the members of your team in the few months following the spiritual Dark Night. I promise you, you'll have a lot of fun doing so.

7. You Will Receive Clear Communication and Guidance

As you exit the spiritual Dark Night of the Soul and continue to cement your routine and protocols, you'll discover your powers of communication with the "other side" amplify. During the early part of your spiritual awakening journey, you must rely on signs, divination, and intuition to receive messages from your team. By the end of your journey, it will be as though you're sitting and talking to your guides in the same room. This is because you're continuing to integrate—effectively building a "channel."

I've found that, not only can I speak to my guides whenever I wish, I can also speak to departed family members and my soul's previous avatars (i.e. the spirits of human incarnations of my soul in previous lives.) Also, once I completed my lessons in judgment, I started to receive clear, direct guidance. My habit is to discuss the situation with the most appropriate guide, examine options, share opinions, and jointly decide on the best route forward.

8. *You Will Make Plans with Your Team*

One great benefit lying in wait on the other side of the spiritual Dark Night of the Soul is the ability to make plans with the help of your team. You'll no longer feel that you're fumbling around in the dark. As long as you're clear about your goals, your team will help you design a plan to achieve them. Once you've agreed your objectives and next steps, your guides can organize things from their elevated viewpoint. As I mentioned before, there are opportunities piled up all around you, just waiting to be activated. With a coherent plan, your team can leverage them more effectively. You get to enjoy a clear sense of direction and have confidence you will succeed.

9. *You Will Enjoy a Clear Sense of Direction*

The preferred approach in "Soul World" is to do "the next bit, then the next bit, then the next bit," because in our fluid universe, where free will reigns supreme, and two teams are conducting opposing missions, the circumstances are always changing. There are always plenty of curve balls coming our way. In the business world, this incremental approach is known as "agile". Rather than planning everything meticulously from beginning to end, you look just a few steps ahead. This means you can adjust as you go, with maximum flexibility.

This is the way your team will encourage you to work, and once you've released attachment to needing a "concrete" view of the entire path ahead of you, you'll find it an effective, satisfying way to proceed. Working in this agile way requires a great deal of faith that things will "shake out." Fortunately, I have seen first-hand how powerful and effective my team is and what they can help make happen, so it's easy for me to believe they'll deliver what I need, as long as I do my part. I am sure you'll be able to develop the same level of trust.

How nice it is to get on with things, knowing that step A will lead to outcome B! After a time, you relax and trust the plan to take you where you need to go, one way or another (and sometimes those ways can be surprising). All you have to do is follow the next few steps on the path you've agreed, knowing things will fall into place. Having this clear sense of direction in your life removes stress, leaving you to get on and enjoy fulfilling your soul's purpose.

10. You Will Know Your Soul's Purpose

You'll probably have gained an inkling of your soul's purpose in the lead up to the spiritual Dark Night of the Soul, but you'll develop a deeper understanding in the period following it. Often, as higher evolved souls, we have multiple purposes. We may not achieve them all in this lifetime—and that's fine—but we should be aware of "Plan A." If we decide not to pursue one or more strands, that's our prerogative. Remember, we have free will.

For my own part I decided not to take one path that was available to me. In the 2000s I had a burgeoning DJ career in London. I was "spotted" by a promoter who wanted to give me a residency in a new super-club in the North of England, playing alongside household names. This is the kind of break amateur DJs can only dream of! After a great deal of thought I declined the offer. I wanted a quiet life where I could enjoy the daylight and work in my garden at weekends. So while this opportunity had been planned for me before my incarnation, in the end, it didn't suit the person I'd become. It's impossible for us to know exactly how our personality will develop during a human lifetime, there are so many influencing factors. That's one reason our team arranges so many different opportunities.

Before I knew my purpose I felt unfulfilled. I asked myself, "Isn't there more than this?!" I felt I had a lot to contribute but didn't know how. Giving my good energy to big business seemed hollow; I felt I was wasting my potential. Exiting the spiritual Dark Night of the Soul and finally understanding what I came to do was a massive relief. Now I'm clear on my purpose (helping others through their spiritual awakenings is just one part of it), I can forge on and make plans with the help of my team, secure in the knowledge that I'm fulfilling my "destiny." It's changed my life.

11. You Will Become Close to Your Higher Self

You may have learned the name of your higher self prior to entering the spiritual Dark Night of the Soul. Our guides convey this through meditation or a similar trance state, such as hypnosis, or in a dream. If not, you should discover it soon (ask the universe to tell you). Either way, you may not have spent much time with them one on one—at least not consciously. Once you exit the spiritual Dark Night, that will change. Your higher self will become your bosom buddy—and rightly so, because they're your constant companion. In fact, they've been guiding you since the day you were born, you just weren't aware.

Why We Naturally Feel Close to Our Higher Selves

Your higher self, or oversoul, is the soul from which you were "birthed." Just as in a human family, you share characteristics with your higher self, passed down to you via your soul DNA. So, when you get to know them, you'll discover you have much in common. In fact, if you're a "bodhisattva" soul (meaning you've completed at least ninety-eight percent of your soul's lessons), you'll find you are almost identical. If, that is, you've shed your Ego and are in "soul mode".

As our souls continue from birth along their eternal lives, accruing lessons, they accumulate qualities and aspects of the member of the Council of Light they descend from on the "soul tree". This is just like the family trees we have on Earth, but for the entire community of souls which exists in our universe. The ten main branches of the soul tree correspond to the ten most senior members of the Council of Light. In other words, we're all descended from one of these beings at soul level. I talk in more detail about the Council of Light and the soul tree on my blog: sophiapersephone.com/sophia-persephone-blog.

So, over successive lifetimes, we become more and more similar to our higher selves, sometimes startlingly so. I remember saying to Sophia when I was getting to know her, "Gosh, you sound a lot like me." At which she rolled her eyes and replied, "Go figure." So that told me! This similarity engenders closeness—the kind of relationship you often see between twins.

12. You Will Discover Your Soul's Name

During the period following the spiritual Dark Night you should also learn your soul's name, if you haven't done so already. Often you will recognize it as a name from myth, religion, or literature. This is deliberate. The names of souls have been woven into earthly traditions since the beginning of time, exactly so we would have points of reference when the time for mass awakening came. (You may recognise my own names—Sophia and Persephone—as coming from Greek myth.) This means we can quickly gain an understanding of our immortal roots, simply by searching the internet. Your soul's name is rarely the name you were given at birth. That is the name of the human "avatar" your soul chose to work with in this lifetime.

You can discover your soul's name through guided meditation or simply ask the question in your own meditation, if you're at the point where you're receiving messages verbally. Some mediums and psychics can also discover this information in the Akashic Records (always work with someone you trust). You will know when you've discovered your true soul's name because it will feel "right."

13. You Will Gain a Deep Understanding of Who You Are

All of this: knowing your purpose, forging a relationship with your higher self, and learning your soul's name, allows you to develop a deep understanding of who you are. When we talk about people being their "authentic selves," what we mean—whether we know it or not—is that someone is behaving in a way which is true to their soul's nature. The farther down the path of spiritual awakening you go, the more authentic you become. In fact, you can't help becoming aware of yourself as an immortal soul and of the abilities and powers within you. It's a wonderful feeling.

14. You Will Develop Heightened Intuition and Empathy

As I've explained, what we call "spiritual awakening" is the process of integration with our higher selves. The more we integrate, the clearer communication becomes—we're building a channel. After a Dark Night, this integration continues. This means we can start to enjoy direct access to the knowledge stored in the higher dimensions (the parts of us that live "up there" have this knowledge at their fingertips all the time). What this means, to an incarnated soul on Earth, is that our "intuition" becomes stronger. We develop a keen sense of "knowing."

This doesn't just apply to ourselves; we also develop stronger intuition about others. When we awaken spiritually, we're able to understand other people on a deeper level. For example, we might know:

- where they descend from on the soul tree;
- what their relationship is to us at soul level;

- where they are on their spiritual journey;
- what their purpose is in this lifetime;
- the challenges they've faced in the past and those they're dealing with now.

In fact, we might know more about someone than they know themselves. This helps us feel empathy. We're able to accept people for who they are, where they've been, and what they're going through. Think about a time in the future when most of humanity will awaken and integrate with their higher selves: we will live in a society vastly different from the one we live in today, full of understanding, tolerance, empathy and compassion.

15. You Will Be Able to Act with Awareness

Once you've passed through the spiritual Dark Night of the Soul (as I know you will), you act with increased awareness. In fact, your guides will encourage you to develop a state of constant mindfulness, an integral feature of spiritual awakening. Rather than allowing your subconscious and Ego to dictate your actions and behaviors, you will operate using your conscious mind. This also gives you the opportunity to break bad habits (in my case, including a twenty-five-year alcohol addiction), and to live your life shackle-free, with intent. I can't tell you how wonderful that is. These days, even when I deviate from the "perfect path," I do so with awareness, cognizant of the consequences. I *decide* to do so. The universe supports this kind of detour, by the way. As I said, it's a keen advocate of the "80/20 rule."

16. You May Gain Powers of Precognition

If you're going through your spiritual awakening, you almost certainly have innate psychic abilities. You may have discovered this at a young age, for example by realizing you had telepathic powers, or could see things others couldn't. While these qualities almost always fade as we grow older, they tend to come back with a vengeance during an awakening. It's possible you may develop "precognition," the ability to see or sense the future. You discover that you "just know" what will happen next, in the short, medium, or long term. These types of people are known as "seers." Many seers will be awakening in the next five years.

17. Your Power of Telepathy Will Increase

Telepathy is the ability to communicate using only your mind. You're doing this every time you talk to your higher self and guides across the dimensions. However, you may find you can do this on the physical plane too, following your exit from the spiritual Dark Night of the Soul (as well as in the "connected" period leading up to it). I find, for example, that often I reply to a question someone has only thought of, rather than articulated. I don't "hear" the question in my mind, but as I speak, I become aware I've picked up a telepathic signal. This realisation often dawns as a result of the surprised expression on the thinker's face! As with all psychic abilities, you can develop this aptitude further if you decide to focus on it.

18. Your Ability to Manifest Will Grow

All of this fantastic work you've been doing on "mind over matter" (because that's what it is) will increase your powers of manifestation exponentially. As part of your spiritual progress, your team will have introduced you to the concept of manifestation—often called the Law of Attraction. You already know the fundamental techniques and have, perhaps, incorporated them into your practice. Once you're through the spiritual Dark Night of the Soul, increase your manifestation efforts. Imagine how powerful this will be in the context of your awakened self. You'll be fully integrated with your higher self, operating with awareness and intuition, know your purpose, have a plan supported by your team, and be manifesting like crazy. In short, there'll be no stopping you. This alone should be enough to keep you focused on getting through the spiritual Dark Night. It's a genuine opportunity to manifest your perfect life, as you want it, full of purpose and opportunity.

19. You Will Get Back into Flow

The upshot of a regular spiritual routine, coupled with the intention to manifest your plan is—you get into flow. You'll already have experienced a period of flow in the phase of awakening before the spiritual Dark Night, during the "connection" stage. The state of flow you experience immediately after the Dark Night is unlikely to be as intense, however, it's still extremely powerful.

After I exited the spiritual Dark Night of the Soul I transformed my life. Not only that, sitting here today, I can already see the threads leading to the future I want for myself, which haven't manifested yet. Yes, there are still niggly aspects to life, but that's the reality of living in this three-dimensional environment and our relatively primitive human society. Typically, as long as I stick to my practice and work to move my plan forward, things "flow". That's my reality and it will be yours too, if you just push on through the spiritual Dark Night and continue to invest in your spiritual progress.

20. You Will Start to Enjoy Your Life a Whole Lot More

Being in flow = a more enjoyable life. Also, once you're out of the spiritual Dark Night, your team will encourage you to have fun. Yes, you can live a spiritual life *and* enjoy yourself! In fact, that's the idea. We're not supposed to be miserable. Think how inspiring you could be to others as a model for how to a simultaneously spiritual and pleasurable existence. And make no mistake, as a higher evolved soul waking up now, you're here to lead by example—that's part of your purpose.

For years I worked a "9 to 5" job (more like "7 to 7"—sixty-hour weeks are the norm in corporate life), even though it didn't suit my body clock at all. I'm an early bird who likes to get on with things as soon as I wake up. Then (ideally) I need an afternoon nap at 3 p.m. to be able to function past 6 p.m. I prefer to work shorter hours, six days a week. However, to have any hope of building a successful career, I had to fit into the rigid pattern dictated by society and big business. Well, not anymore.

Now I work when I want, on the things I enjoy. Ironically, I still work a sixty-hour week (occasionally more), but in a way that fits my natural rhythm. Sometimes I take an afternoon nap, but sometimes I choose to sunbathe on my terrace high in the Andalusian mountains, or take a dip in the hot tub or pool. This is the life I've chosen, and I'm happier and healthier for it. Am I lucky? You bet! But I created my luck. I knew what I wanted, and with the help of my team, I made it happen. I now enjoy life a great deal and, to the delight of my team, I'm relaxed and content. That's what's waiting for you on the other side of the spiritual Dark Night of the Soul (including the hot tub and pool—if that's what you want).

21. You Will Have a Greater Opportunity to Help Others

If you're going through a spiritual awakening right now, you're here to serve. Not only that, but your service will almost certainly be on a "macro" level. You'll find big, impactful ways to help people (or animals, or the planet). Maybe you'll set up a business, write a book, or become a motivational speaker, sharing your ideas and experience. Perhaps you'll be a campaigner…? A social media influencer…? A performer….? Perhaps you'll patent an invention that helps the whole of humanity. Maybe all of the above! You already know you are here to help, or you sense this is true.

Once you're out of the spiritual Dark Night and possess all the incredible abilities outlined in this chapter, you can pursue this goal with intent and focus. Not only that, you'll intuit how best you can serve, and then work with your team to build a plan to get there. There's nothing more satisfying than helping others or contributing to the greater good. To my mind, this is one of the most significant benefits of spiritual awakening.

22. You Have the Opportunity to be a Force for Change

As well as helping others, you'll be a veritable force for wider change. And let's be honest, the Earth needs it. We're right at the start of a huge, global, societal shift, so as an early awakener, you're already a pioneer. Even just talking about your awakening to people you meet (once you know they're receptive) makes you a changemaker. Not to mention the brilliant, trailblazing ideas you may have. It's satisfying and humbling to know you can leave a legacy and that you might, in this life, help shift humanity toward a better future. Oh, and if you're wondering if you're up to the task—you are.

23. You Will Attain Full Integration with Your Higher Self

If you push through the spiritual Dark Night of the Soul and attain 100 percent integration with your higher self, you'll discover you have the ability to function at your highest potential. You'll regain your full soul power while on the earthly plane. In addition, at 100 percent integration, you'll be able to ease up a little on your daily ritual—you go into maintenance mode. That will give you more time to focus on your purpose and plan. If you're wondering how you'll know if you're fully integrated, don't worry, your team will tell you. It's a cause for celebration, especially since you'll be one of the few people on the planet who've made it so far. Congratulations!

24. Ultimately You Will Achieve Transcendence

When my team told me I'd reached full integration with Sophia, I assumed that was the end of my spiritual awakening journey. But I soon discovered, there's one last stage—transcendence. During transcendence, we learn to use the "channel" we built during integration. While you were integrating, your team "came down" to you. Transcendence means you rise up to them. By the end of the transcendence phase, you can operate on the physical plane as your higher self—with the astounding benefits that brings—using your superconscious mind rather than your conscious mind.

Then, you no longer need to ask your team for guidance because you can access all the information you need yourself, by consulting the Akashic Records—the vast universal database. The ultimate intention is that you become so adept at understanding and using the various compartments of the mind that you can switch in and out of modalities as you wish. You can move between human, soul, and higher self "mode." That means you can select whichever state is appropriate for the task in hand—including choosing to enjoy yourself in pure, physical "human mode" from time to time.

Summary of Benefits

In this chapter, I've listed twenty-four wonderful skills and benefits which come with exiting the spiritual Dark Night of the Soul. I'm sure there are more. If you're undergoing this kind of Dark Night, hopefully this gives you incentive enough to keep going. I promise you it's worth every depressing, dull, disconnected, despairing moment. Below I've listed all twenty-four benefits as a brief reminder. If you're going through a spiritual Dark Night, please bookmark this page and read this list when you need to remember why you're doing this, and why you should work to push on through. The more of us who do, the more we can help and encourage others to do the same.

It's no exaggeration to say we have the power to transform the World this way.

1. You will learn to detach;
2. You will develop better judgement;
3. Your confidence will increase;
4. You will gain proficiency in spiritual techniques;
5. You will establish a daily spiritual routine;
6. You will develop a new type of relationship with your guides;
7. You will receive clear communication and guidance;
8. You will make plans with your team;
9. You will enjoy a clear sense of direction;
10. You will finally know your soul's purpose;
11. You will become close to your higher self;
12. You will discover your soul's name;
13. You will gain a deep understanding of who you are;
14. You will develop heightened intuition and empathy;
15. You will be able to act with awareness;
16. You may gain powers of precognition;
17. Your power of telepathy will increase;
18. Your ability to manifest will grow;
19. You will get back into flow;
20. You will start to enjoy your life a whole lot more;
21. You will have a greater opportunity to help others;
22. You have the opportunity to be a force for change;
23. You will attain full integration with your higher self;
24. Ultimately you will achieve transcendence.

Part II:

Protocols for Getting Through a Dark Night of the Soul

Chapter 5—An Overview of the Protocols

Introduction

It's spring. I'm sitting in bed staring at the wall, overwhelmed by a sense of desolation and loss. I want to cry but I don't have the energy. I feel angry, frustrated, and alone. It seems as though I'm stuck in a never-ending void, abandoned by those I had come to trust and rely on. There's no point to anything. This describes my state when I was deep in the throes of my first spiritual Dark Night of the Soul, catatonic to all external appearances, but raging inside with resentment. No wonder I failed to dig myself out.

Fortunately, after that first attempt at getting through the spiritual Dark Night, as I explained, my team gave me protocols to help me succeed on my second try. ("Protocols" is the word they use and so I have adopted it.) These are the techniques I'm going to share with you in this section of the book. They work. Whether you're going through a growth-oriented or spiritual Dark Night, or you just want to get farther along the spiritual path, adopting even a few of these practices will help you.

I promise these protocols will work for anyone and everyone. They are exactly the tools you need to get through a spiritual depression. Try to stick to them as close to 100 percent as you can, and develop a daily routine. That's your shortest path out of a Dark Night.

Many of these protocols are not specific to the Dark Night of the Soul, but I wanted to include them so this book can continue to be useful to you once you're through the other side. Taken together, these protocols represent a comprehensive catalogue of spiritual techniques and behaviors—a toolkit for awakening, whichever stage of the journey you're at. As you start to embed them into your routine, you'll notice that your state of mind and life improves. They're all you need to transform your existence and create the reality you wish for yourself.

The Six Categories of Protocols

In this section of the book I provide forty protocols, tried and tested, which fall into six categories. These are:

1) Mindset
2) Healthy Living
3) Spiritual Practice
4) Self-Development
5) Creative Pursuits
6) Giving Back

You don't need to adopt every practice; that would be a lot! But I wanted to give you plenty of options so you can find a formula that works for you. Please feel free to choose the protocols you feel most drawn towards, but don't forget the basics—daily meditation being the most notable example. Bear in mind it will be more effective to pick a few protocols and stick with them for a period of time, than to try every one for just a day or two.

The Importance of Meditation

Without a regular meditation practice (by which I mean *daily*), you will not progress. It's an essential tool, and if you're going through a spiritual Dark Night, there's no substitute. If you're going through a growth-oriented Dark Night, regular meditation will make a huge difference to your mood and circumstances. Even if you're not experiencing a Dark Night, meditation is a strong foundation of happy, healthy living for all incarnated souls—every one of us benefits from meditating daily. So, if you do nothing else, set time aside for this protocol (there are simple, easy ways to do it, which I will explain in Protocol 16).

You Can Do It!

Remember, the universe never gives us anything we can't handle. You are an exceptionally old, incredibly strong soul, on an empowering and liberating path. Yes, you have to fight your way through a difficult period, but it's temporary. Your team has led you to this book and these protocols, exactly so you can get through the Dark Night of the Soul—as you intended to before you incarnated in this life. You. Can. Do. It.

Chapter 6—Mindset Protocols

Time to adjust your set. It's amazing how altering your attitude and thought patterns can lift your mood and move you forward. These Mindset Protocols help you reprogramme your thinking patterns for positivity.

***

Protocol 1: Accept the Situation You Are In

The first time I went through the spiritual Dark Night of the Soul, I didn't want to believe what was happening, even though my team told me plainly I was in the Dark Night. I couldn't accept it and avoided doing the things I needed to do. On one level I think I believed it would all just magically go away.

Possibly the biggest factor in my success on the second attempt was acceptance. I now understood the Dark Night was unavoidable and I had to make my way through for the good of myself, my team, and the mission. Therefore, I approached it differently. Although I still felt low, disconnected, and lethargic, I forced myself to embrace the experience. I stuck to a daily spiritual routine and doubled down on my efforts.

Knowing I was doing what I needed to do—and understanding it was just a matter of time before I was out of the woods—made everything easier. This is as true of a growth-oriented Dark Night as a spiritual one. *Everything is a process.* If you have suffered multiple depressive episodes in your life (growth-oriented Dark Nights of the Soul), you already know this. When a low hits, you have to accept that is where you're at, at that moment in time, and do the things you know from experience will alleviate your condition. Unless we accept where we are, it's hard to move forward.

At its most extreme, acceptance here means being grateful for the Dark Night of the Soul. This isn't as crazy as it sounds. The Dark Night is an opportunity to pick up new skills and learn something about yourself—including how resilient you are. If you can make this (admittedly hard) "head switch," everything else will come more easily.

Exercise: Build Acceptance

Stand in front of a mirror and calm your mind with a few deep breaths. Look yourself in the eyes and repeat three times, "I am grateful for the Dark Night of the Soul and everything it's teaching me". Do this daily, or whenever you feel you need a lift.

***

Protocol 2: Remember What's Waiting for You on the Other Side

If you're in a spiritual Dark Night of the Soul, keep your eyes on the prize. In Chapter 4 I listed twenty-four wonderful benefits waiting for you on the other side of the Dark Night. Whenever you want to give up: *Read. The. List.*

You can also cast your mind back to the time leading up to the Dark Night when you enjoyed the deepest possible connection to your guides and the universe. Remember how wonderful that was? That's what you're working towards as you continue to integrate with your higher self.

If you're in a growth-oriented Dark Night, try to remember the last time you felt happy. In your mind, re-experience the lightness which comes with releasing energetic blockages in your system. That is what's waiting for you and what these protocols will help you recover.

Exercise: Remember What's Waiting for You

Lie down in a comfortable position, somewhere you won't be disturbed. Close your eyes. Cast your mind back to the last time you felt happy (growth-oriented Dark Night) or the period of connection you enjoyed before the Dark Night descended (spiritual Dark Night). Recreate the feelings and sensations of that time in your mind. Allow yourself to relax and enjoy them. Tell yourself, "This is what is waiting for me on the other side of the Dark Night".

***

Protocol 3: Be Kind to Yourself

It's essential you're kind to yourself during the Dark Night of the Soul. There are two main ways you can show kindness to yourself during this period. The first: cut yourself some slack. Yes, it's desirable to stick to your protocol routine 100 percent of the time, but you're not a machine. You will have good days and bad days. If you "fall off the wagon," don't worry. It happens. Just get back on the next day and start again. It's your journey. You decide how you want to do it.

The second way you can be kind to yourself is by giving yourself permission to do things you enjoy, perhaps things you wouldn't normally do. Longing to stay in your pyjamas all day? Go for it! (Just not every day). Desperate to binge on a new Netflix series? Be my guest. Want to splurge on a new tech gadget, or luxurious bubbles for your bath? Just. Do. It. The words of John Lennon's "Whatever Gets

You Thru the Night" come to mind. Yes, I promise you, it will be all right.

Exercise: Treat Yourself

Write a list of things you can do to be kind to yourself. Include some small, medium, and large things. When you need a pick-me-up, choose something from the list. Give yourself full permission to enjoy it.

***

Protocol 4: Rest—a Lot

Resting During the Spiritual Dark Night of the Soul

During the Dark Night of the Soul you'll need to get comfortable with the idea that you need to rest. In the case of the spiritual Dark Night, tiredness can be severe, similar to chronic fatigue syndrome, depending on the degree to which your chakras are constricted.

Fortunately, our teams usually arrange matters so we can take time out to deal with this part of the spiritual awakening journey. Superficially, what they arrange may feel negative. For example, my team imposed a period of rest on me in the following way: I lost my job because of the COVID-19 pandemic and contracted a nasty case of Coronavirus in the very first month of the crisis that turned into "Long Covid." That laid me out for quite a while. But boy, was I grateful I didn't have to work when the Dark Night of the Soul fell upon me! If you're going through the spiritual Dark Night, your team has probably arranged something for you. If not, please carve out as much time as you can to rest. Don't feel bad about it. If you have family or partnership commitments, explain that you might not be up to much for a while. Ask for their support.

People I've coached through their own spiritual Dark Nights confirm they've had this experience of enforced downtime, and Sophia asked me to emphasise the need for rest in this book. So, expect to feel tired, expect to need (a lot) more sleep than usual, and accept this is part of the process. The more you can sleep, the more beneficial it will be to you, and the more quickly you will traverse the spiritual Dark Night of the Soul. There's no need to feel guilty.

Resting During the Growth-Oriented Dark Night of the Soul

Tiredness can accompany the growth-oriented Dark Night of the Soul, however it's rarely as severe as during the spiritual Dark Night, unless your solar plexus chakra is significantly blocked (the seat of drive and energy), or all of your chakras are in very poor health. Because you're not in a "formal process" as with the spiritual Dark Night, your team is less likely to arrange circumstances around your condition. This is because they need to allow things to become "bad enough" to force change. As long as you're making steps towards the changes you need, your team will be able to assist you. In this case, if you need rest, they will facilitate it.

***

Protocol 5: Take One Day at a Time

If you've ever taken part in an endurance sport (marathon running is an excellent example), you know that the best way to get to the finish line is to focus on putting one foot in front of another. If you're looking ahead constantly to all those miles you have to complete, it soon starts to feel insurmountable. The Dark Night of the Soul is the same. If you think about it stretching out into the distant future, you're likely to get demoralized.

The best thing to do is focus on getting through each day. The spiritual Dark Night follows an extremely specific pattern. It operates at a constant level most of the time, with a sudden uptick at the end when the universe reopens your chakras and energy starts to flow once more. That means you have no indication that it's about to lift. You literally become aware something is changing around 24 hours ahead of it ending. If you keep wondering how much further you have to go, it will be harder for you to focus on getting through. Instead, just do what you can each day, knowing it's all adding up, even if you can't "feel" it. Once you're a few weeks in, you can ask your guides how long they think you have left. There's no guarantee you'll get an answer, but they can communicate with you from time to time during a spiritual Dark Night, so give it a go.

A growth-oriented Dark Night of the Soul behaves differently. Improvement comes gradually. You may see no effect whatsoever for the first two or three weeks, depending on the severity of the blockage you are trying to shift. However, if you're doing the right things and making the necessary changes, after that, bit by bit, things should improve. In some ways, this makes the process easier than with the spiritual Dark Night of the Soul because you start to see light at the end of the tunnel. Taking things day by day is still important, so you don't try to run before you can walk, or get disheartened and slip backwards.

***

Protocol 6: Decide to Succeed

Did you know you can "decide" to succeed? It's a genuine thing. Even when you're at a low ebb, you can state your determination to not let the Dark Night of the Soul beat you. This signals to the universe (and the various parts of your mind) that you intend to get through the Dark Night and failure is not an option. By adopting this attitude, you manifest your success. Holding on to the belief that you can and will get through it will literally help make it happen.

Dealing With Thoughts of Failure

It's natural to have doubts along the way. It's a tough journey. There will be times when you wonder, "Can I do this?" (You can.) When you catch yourself having thoughts of failure, you can replace them with positive statements, so you continue to manifest the success you deserve. You're reprogramming your mind in real time. Here's an example:

Step 1:

You slide into a negative thought pattern: "I hate this! How much longer is it going to last? I don't know if I can continue, maybe I should just give up...."

Step 2:

You notice the negative thought (practicing mindfulness throughout the day will help you with this);

Step 3:

You replace the negative thought with a positive statement—for example: "I intend to live a happy and fulfilling life, and I refuse to let this beat me. I'm having a bad day, but tomorrow will be better. I will get through this Dark Night and out the other side."

After you've done this a few times you will find the negative thoughts occur less frequently.

State Your Intention to Succeed

You can also start each morning by stating your intention to succeed. Incorporate this into your daily ritual. It's important to make an explicit statement of intent, as we did in step 3 of the technique above.

It's best to set your intentions after you've meditated, when your mind is clear and focused. Try something like:

> *"Today I intend to continue to make my way through this Dark Night of the Soul. Each day I will get farther until I'm out the other side. I will not let the Dark Night beat me. I will succeed."*

Feel free to write your own affirmation. State your intention in a way that feels natural to you. It will surprise you how much this speeds your recovery.

Exercise: Intend to Succeed

Write down your intention to succeed in clear lettering on a piece of paper. Make sure to explicitly state that you will not let the Dark Night of the Soul beat you and you will get through it. Pin the piece of paper somewhere where you will see it at least a few times a day.

***

Chapter 7—Healthy Living Protocols

Part of the spiritual awakening journey is learning how to balance the needs of the physical, mental, and spiritual parts of your system ("mind, body, spirit"). Without a healthy physical system, it's difficult to progress. These healthy living protocols will help you get through the Dark Night of the Soul but are important at every stage of the awakening journey.

Don't worry. I'm not advocating that you live like a monk, but there are things you can do that will make an enormous difference to your progress. Some of them are even enjoyable. Please try to embrace a healthy lifestyle so you can build a strong physical platform for the remainder of your awakening journey.

***

Protocol 7: Get Rid of Addictive Substances

Anything that exerts an ongoing influence over your body steals power from your conscious mind. This makes it harder for you to connect to your higher self, or superconscious. You are "anchored" in the physical. This is the polar opposite of what you're trying to do during a Dark Night of the Soul. Some substances are particularly detrimental. These are (in order of impact):

- alcohol;
- hard drugs (excluding psychedelics);

- refined sugar, and
- caffeine.

Even if you're not strongly addicted to any of these but you consume them regularly, they will slow down your progress through the Dark Night. Alcohol is especially damaging, particularly as it's all around us and difficult to avoid, at least in the West.

The Problem with Alcohol

As with everything on Earth, alcohol serves a purpose. Sophia tells me the universe designed it to allow human beings (and some animals) the opportunity to disconnect from their body during times of extreme emotional pain, such as bereavement. It works because alcohol is a sedative. It puts the body to "sleep" and so decreases our feeling of the negative emotions stored in this part of the human system.

At the same time, it stimulates the release of serotonin, the substance which aids connection to our higher selves. Serotonin allows the conscious mind to detach and rise to join the superconscious. That's why we feel euphoric when we're drunk—we're distanced from the negative emotions contained in the body, and connected to our positive higher soul emotions.

However, the clever universe put a safeguard in place, to prevent us from choosing to get drunk all the time (it's nice "up there," so it's understandable we enjoy the release that alcohol gives us). Once the effects of drinking have worn off, we suffer a serotonin "crash". Our reserves are depleted and this causes anxiety and depression, because we're no longer able to ascend and experience the "lightening" which occurs when we draw closer to our higher selves. Depression and anxiety will worsen over time if we continue to drink: this is designed as a deterrent.

So, alcohol is intended by the universe to be taken infrequently, but unfortunately its use has become increasingly pervasive, at least in the Western World. It's interesting that a large proportion of Gen Z chooses not to drink[iii]. This generation is incarnating with an increased natural ability to connect to the higher dimensions, as part of the mass global awakening initiative. They don't "need" alcohol in the same way as older generations for serotonin release, as they're already hyper-connected (although not necessarily consciously).

As a onetime alcoholic, I'm definitely not lecturing anyone about their drinking habits. We're all adults and can make our own decisions. What I can tell you is that, after ten years of repeated depressive episodes (all more or less untreatable), when I stopped drinking, within a month I felt like a different person. A dark black cloud lifted. I wish someone had told me years ago how badly alcohol affects your mental health. But this seems to be something people either don't know, or don't want to talk about.

If you're going through a Dark Night, whether spiritual or growth-oriented, the last thing you need is something that brings down your mood. If you're not experiencing a Dark Night but you wish to follow the path of conscious spiritual awakening, alcohol won't help you. So, if you drink (and especially if you drink every day), I suggest you stop or cut down. As someone who embraced sobriety after thirty years of alcohol abuse, I'm a thousand times happier, calmer, and more relaxed than I was when I drank.

Hard Drugs

Some hard drugs have a similar effect on long-term mental health, and for similar reasons. Cocaine and amphetamines are particularly detrimental, so if you're using these, again, I recommend you stop.

Other drugs, those with psychedelic properties, such as magic mushrooms (psilocybin), ecstasy, ketamine, and cannabis, do not have the same harmful effects and can be beneficial as therapeutic and spiritual tools. However, anything which you come to depend on is detrimental because it takes power from your conscious mind.

If you decide to take psychedelic drugs for whatever reason (please do so safely and legally), that's your prerogative. I talk more about this in Protocol 15.

Quitting Drugs and Alcohol

If you discover you have a problem while you're trying to quit alcohol or drugs, don't feel bad. These are powerful substances which create a temporary link to the higher dimensions, and that's why they feel so "good". However that doesn't mean they're "good for you". As part of the spiritual awakening journey you'll eventually have to relinquish your attachment to external substances and rely on your internal abilities to connect. There are many organisations and online support groups aimed at helping people overcome addiction. If you need help, I recommend seeking them out.

Sugar and Caffeine

It's not just drugs and alcohol that are toxic to your body or habit-forming. Sugar and caffeine are both highly addictive and bad news for your system. If you can cut down (or cut out) these substances, you will increase your ability to connect to your higher self. If you're going through a spiritual Dark Night, you will exit it more quickly. If you're going through a growth-oriented Dark Night, once you are through the initial withdrawal, your mood will lift exponentially. Please note: the natural sugars occurring in fruit and honey are fine.

Sugar and caffeine withdrawal can be difficult to get through. Often people experience something similar to the flu, accompanied by a severe headache. For this reason, it's best to tackle one at a time. Give yourself a few weeks for each and, if you're struggling, gradually reduce your intake rather than going "cold turkey". You'll find your craving and taste for these substances diminish substantially once you've gone without for a while.

Exercise: Beat Your Addictions

Make a list of all the substances you have a dependence on. Rank them in order of severity. Decide whether you are ready to start tackling the list. If so, choose which one to work on first. (Pro tip: if you are giving up alcohol, address this before reducing your sugar intake. You may need sugar to help beat your alcohol cravings.) Once you have decided which dependency you're going to work on, make a plan. Write down what you will do to reduce or eliminate your reliance on the substance. Research techniques and/or organisations which can help you before putting your plan into action.

***

Protocol 8: Eat a "Spiritual" Diet

What do I mean by a "spiritual" diet? Purely that you consume foods that are beneficial in helping you to connect to the universe and avoid ones that aren't. As I mentioned in the previous protocol ("Get Rid of Addictive Substances"), alcohol, refined sugar, and caffeine are all detrimental to spiritual health, so the less you take in of these, the better. The same goes for processed foods, which place a toxic load on the body, and are frequently full of sugar, rooting you to the physical. Red meat and dairy, especially from cows, also inhibit spiritual connection.

As I'm sure you know, you should eat a healthy, vitamin-and-mineral-rich, unprocessed diet, with an emphasis on organic fruits, vegetables, and (ancient) whole grains. While it's preferable to eat no meat at all, some types are beneficial during the Dark Night of the Soul. These are chicken and turkey. There's a substance in the skin of both these birds called tryptophan which helps us produce serotonin.

Serotonin is a vital compound for both physical and spiritual health and helps you connect to the universe. If your preference is to eat no meat at all, I recommend taking a good tryptophan supplement, at least while you're experiencing an episode of the Dark Night.

Do I Need to be Vegan?

Let me dispel one myth—a spiritual diet does not have to be a vegan diet. However, if you are vegan and this way of eating is working for you, great, just continue. The fact is, a vegan diet doesn't work for everyone. Instead the emphasis should be on limiting our reliance on animal products, reducing our intake as much as we can.

Cultural Attitudes to Eating Meat Are Changing

In our contemporary society, it's largely still acceptable to eat animals, in fact, meat is often central to "celebration" meals and traditions. The universe understands it's a lot to expect people to resist such a strong cultural lure. Instead, it asks us to reduce harm. This means, where possible, buying local, organic produce and yes, cutting out as much meat, fish, and dairy as you are able, without impacting your health. Don't beat yourself up if you struggle with this. And again, the 80/20 rule is acceptable. In fact, the 80/20 principle has been adopted in the modern "flexitarian" diet.

In future society, as we progress towards global enlightenment, eating animals or animal products will be considered abhorrent. It'll become culturally taboo. We can already see this move away from animal food sources starting to happen, particularly with the broad selection of meat substitute products now available, and advances being made in lab-grown meat production. So, by default, future generations will not eat animals. Our genes and bodies will adjust, and there will be an ever-increasing number of ways to get everything we need from our food, without having to harm other creatures. In the meantime, do the best you can.

The Mediterranean and Anti-inflammatory Diets

If you're someone who prefers to follow a "diet," there are two ways of eating in particular that are ideal for physical, mental, and spiritual health. One is the traditional Mediterranean diet[iv], which came to prominence in the 1970s. We recognize it today as being close to optimal in terms of human health. The other is the anti-inflammatory or alkaline diet. This is less well known but shares similarities with the Mediterranean diet and is often recommended to people with chronic health conditions, such as rheumatoid arthritis.

One of the best protocols for the anti-inflammatory diet I have found is from a holistic practitioner named Zita West. She developed it as a detox diet for fertility, but it works just as well for spiritual health. If you're interested in discovering more, here's a link to the relevant page on Zita's website: https://www.zitawest.com/5-day-detox/[v]. She has a book too. One of the great "side-benefits" of both diets, particularly if you give Zita's five-day detox a go, is that they result in weight loss, should you need it.

How Much Food Is Enough?

While humans need food to live, we don't actually need very much of it. Think of our ancestors covering vast distances on foot with nothing but a pouch of roots, nuts, and berries to sustain them. It's possible to do a lot with a little. Today we have the habit of eating large meals, three times a day. For most of us, it's too much. On top of this, excess sugar and added chemicals in the modern human diet, toxins in our ecosystem, and the habit of snacking, all cause us to both put on weight *and* feel the need to eat more. Great for "Big Food," bad for us. If you move to an organic, low sugar and refined carbohydrate diet, full of fruit and veg, and eat mindfully, only when you're hungry, you'll soon discover you need far less food than people typically eat in today's society.

Fasting

If you're going through a spiritual Dark Night of the Soul, then fasting might be too much for you right now. However, I wanted to include it because it's such a beneficial and important practice. Perhaps bookmark this page and return to it when you're through. If you're experiencing a growth-oriented Dark Night, then fasting may help. The only way you'll know is to try it and monitor the effects.

Consuming any food roots you in the physical, at least temporarily, while your body is digesting it. Eating frequently means your digestive system is always processing something. More food = more difficulty connecting to your higher self. This is one reason fasting is a spiritual protocol found in all major world religions. By limiting the amount your body needs to do, it provides the conditions for your conscious mind to detach and ascend. Another reason fasting is important to spiritual progress is that it triggers "autophagy," the body's inbuilt system of repair. At a fundamental level, fasting allows you to self-heal. The healthier your body is, the less it needs to do and the more your mind can transcend. Also, if you have weight to lose, fasting will help. This doesn't need to be extreme, you can use intermittent fasting or "time-restricted eating." Doctor Michael Mosely is an advocate of this approach so if you'd like to learn more, his website is a good place to start[vi].

Longer Fasts

Personally, I have used a fasting practice known as OMAD[vii], which helped me lose nearly thirty pounds. It stands for "One Meal a Day," which means you fast for around twenty-four hours between eating windows. I used to eat this way every other day. It's much easier than it sounds, as long as you build up to it and focus on the right foods. I have also found multi-day fasts to be beneficial in terms of weight loss, spiritual connection, and overall energy. My longest was a three day water fast (during which you consume only water and herbal teas). It was difficult, but by the end, I seemed to connect more powerfully to the universe and my higher self. However, this isn't a fast for beginners. If you want to give it a go, check with your doctor first, or look into one of the centers in the UK, Europe, and the U.S., where you can undertake medically supervised multi-day fasts. Please note that anyone with a history of eating disorders shouldn't embark upon a fast without appropriate supervision.

Exercise: Try Fasting

(This exercise is only for those with no history of eating disorders.) Experiment with intermittent fasting for one week or, if you're already using this protocol, progress to a longer fast, safely and with supervision if required. Document the impact your fasting behavior has on your level of connection to the universe and your overall mood and sense of well-being.

***

Protocol 9: Take Supplements

Whatever type of diet you're eating, you probably need additional nutrients. This is because food today is less nutrient-dense than it was, even a few decades ago. We have to eat more to get what we need but, as we learned in the previous protocol, the aim is to reduce the amount of food we consume. This creates a gap which can be filled by high quality supplements.

Which supplements are required depends on the individual. I took guidance from my team, so if your communication channel is nice and open, ask them what you need. For me, it was tryptophan, magnesium, a good all-round multi-vitamin, l-tyrosine, l-lysine, and Omega 3. I needed all of these for a few months, particularly while I was giving up alcohol. Now I just take magnesium and a multi-vitamin each day which seem to do the job. If you can't yet connect to your team to ask for advice, it's worth meeting with a qualified nutritionist. Of course, if you feel full of beans and everything works as it should, continue as you are—you're doing something right.

CBD Oil

Another supplement my team recommended for me was CBD oil, which is legal in the UK and across most of the U.S., Canada, and Europe. Now I'm fully integrated and transcended, I don't need it, but I was grateful for it when I was going through the Dark Night of the Soul. CBD oil is derived from cannabis but has no psychoactive properties. In other words, you won't get high. This is useful because you can take it throughout the day when you need to. For example, it's excellent at soothing symptoms of anxiety.

Because CBD oil helps you to connect more easily to the higher dimensions, for some people, it can relieve severe detrimental mental and emotional states, such as depression, PTSD, and chronic insomnia. This miraculous liquid has many benefits, so rather than list them all, here's a link to a useful Forbes article that tells you all you need to know about this wonderful supplement: https://www.forbes.com/health/body/cbd-oil-benefits/[viii]. Buy organic if you can afford it (but don't worry if you can't).

***

Protocol 10: Spend Time in Nature

Human beings are part of nature and designed to co-exist with it as part of Earth's symbiotic ecology. The more time you can spend in the great outdoors, the better, spiritually speaking. It's well documented that regular excursions into the natural world have a positive impact on mental health. Good mental health = good spiritual health. The reason spending time in nature is so beneficial is that there's an energy exchange which takes place between us and our surroundings.

The natural world absorbs negative energy from us and bestows positive energy—it's a lot like photosynthesis. It's one reason you feel invigorated after a walk in the country—you've received an energetic "top-up." Your chakras have expanded, blockages have been at least partly cleared, and you have increased energy flow. Taking up gardening has the same effect plus, as a bonus, you can grow lovely organic veggies and fruits. However, the benefit derived from being out in nature is temporary (remember the twenty-four-hour cycle), so it's important to have a routine that involves spending time away from the city and out in the beautiful landscape, wherever you are.

Exercise: Get Out in Nature

Take a look at your weekly schedule and identify at least two opportunities to get out in Nature. If you're already spending some time every week outdoors, see if there's a way to get into Nature daily. When you're out in the landscape, don't forget to hug a tree.

***

Protocol 11: Spend Time in Water

Water is also exceptionally beneficial to the human system. The more time you can spend in or near water the better, be it the ocean, a lake, a river, or a swimming pool (salt water is preferable to chlorinated). In fact, deriving benefit from water can be as simple as taking a bath or a shower, if that's all you have available. If so, why not invest in some essential oils and treat yourself to a nice, long soak? You will always feel better afterwards.

Water is beneficial for two reasons:

- it helps your energy flow, which is one reason we feel restored after a bath, shower, or swim, and
- it grounds your body, which frees your conscious mind to ascend.

As we now know, when our body feels secure, it allows us to rise up and connect to the higher dimensions. If you can incorporate a regular dip into your routine, you'll feel the benefits instantly. The current trend toward wild and ocean swimming offer the perfect opportunity. (It's no coincidence these have become popular right at the start of the mass awakening.)

Exercise: Spend Time in Water

Schedule a swim, treat yourself to a long, pampering bath, or jump in the hot tub, (see, I told you some of these protocols would be enjoyable!).

***

Protocol 12: Head for the Sun

The spirit of the Architect, the builder of our universe, is embodied in our sun. It's literally the "light of the World." Therefore, any time spent (safely) in the sun's rays will top up your physical, mental, and spiritual reserves—which is exactly what you need during an episode of the Dark Night of the Soul. If you're lucky enough to live somewhere with plenty of this glorious resource, put time aside to spend in it. You don't need to be "active," just sunbathing is fine. Even better, meditate in the sunshine. However briefly, the benefit is exponential.

If you don't live in a sunny locale, then consider investing in a sun lamp, and take your holidays in sunny locations if you can.

***

Protocol 13: Practice Yoga and Other Forms of Gentle Exercise

It's no secret that regular exercise is good for your physical and mental health. It builds strength and stamina, and pumps oxygen around your body. Sophia tells me that oxygen is a vehicle for positive energy, so increasing oxygen flow in your system brings spiritual benefits. This is one reason yoga is so beneficial, focusing as it does on the breath.

If you dislike working out, there's good news. You don't have to get hot and sweaty to reap the benefits. In fact, I guarantee there is some kind of exercise you enjoy. Cast your mind back to when you were a child. What activities did you love? Somewhere in there is something you can consider "exercise." If you're inactive, I encourage you to "find the thing" that gets you up and out of your chair. For me, it's hiking. I love to walk. It gives me an opportunity to get close to nature and clear my mind. For you, it might be going to the gym or cycling, or doing Pilates. Or, it might be dancing, walking the dog, messing around with your kids, playing active video games, gardening, paint balling, or having sex. These all count as exercise.

The Magic of Yoga

Yoga is particularly good for us. All forms of yoga help bring mind, body, and spirit back into balance. It's meditative (as many forms of solo exercise are), so it helps you build and strengthen your connection to the universe and your higher self, both on a temporary and foundational basis. This is enormously helpful during a Dark Night, whichever type you're experiencing. Also, as I mentioned, it increases the influx of good energy into your body via oxygen in the breath.

If you haven't tried yoga, or you haven't got into it properly, I recommend giving it a go. There are plenty of excellent resources on the internet. I use Adriene's videos on YouTube at home. They're very enjoyable and accessible to all levels. Here's a link to her channel: https://www.youtube.com/c/yogawithadriene[ix].

Recommended Forms of Exercise During the Dark Night of the Soul

As well as yoga, walking or running in nature and swimming, are all immensely helpful during a Dark Night of the Soul. They bring you into contact with either the outdoors world or with water, and they increase the flow of oxygen through your body. If you combine these activities with meditation, then you're doubling the positive impact. In fact, walking meditation is one of the most beneficial practices a human being can adopt, whether or not they're in the Dark Night of the Soul.

Of course, if you're feeling low on energy because of the Dark Night, just take it easy and only exercise if you feel up to it. Sometimes a gentle ten minute walk is all we can manage, and that's fine. If you listen to your body, it will guide you. Just try not to become completely inactive.

Exercise: Get Active

Put aside half an hour or an hour to do some kind of physical activity. Pick something you know you enjoy or which you haven't done before. If possible, combine it with meditation.

***

Protocol 14: Get a Pet

Human beings and animals are supposed to co-exist. Yes, we're their guardians, but they are also *our* protectors, doctors, and teachers. Not everyone can have a pet, but if you're able to, please consider this avenue as a route to spiritual health. Cats and dogs in particular are "designed" to assist us in myriad ways. It's why they have become domesticated over the centuries. It's all part of the unified universal system within which every living thing exists.

One of the principal ways our four-legged friends help us is that they (as with everything in nature) facilitate an energy exchange, drawing out negative energy and imparting positive energy. Cats are especially "absorbent" in this way, as the ancient Egyptians understood so well. If you have a cat and train it to lie on you while you meditate, you'll find it enhances your practice and ability to connect. All of my cats—Minnie, Dali, and Morris—are aware of my spiritual routine and, nine times out of ten, one of them will come and snooze on my stomach during my morning meditation. It's enjoyable for both of us and makes a difference to the level of connection I experience.

If you can't accommodate a dog or a cat, adding a smaller pet to your household is still beneficial: hamsters, guinea pigs, rats, birds, reptiles, and so on, are all great additions to your family. Just make sure you give them the home they deserve and can afford to look after them properly (the universe will help you with money if you need it, especially if you're investing in your spiritual journey). If you can't find space for an animal, there are still ways to spend time with other creatures. Perhaps you have friends with pets, your neighbor has a dog you can offer to walk, or you can volunteer at an animal shelter. Besides the physical, mental, and spiritual benefits spending time with an animal brings, it's an opportunity for you to do something for them. By looking after others—animals included—and putting their needs before our own, we can make huge spiritual leaps.

Exercise: Spend Time with Animals

Consciously plan time to spend in the company of animals, your own or someone else's. Play, cuddle, communicate and feel your spirits lift.

***

Protocol 15: Investigate Psychedelic Therapies

I know this is a divisive area, largely because psychedelics received panic-mongering press during the 1960s. However, ideas and research have both moved on and I urge you to read the latest literature concerning these incredible substances and their therapeutic uses. Among other things, the correct and controlled use of psychedelics can help with:

- PTSD (Post-Traumatic Stress Disorder);
- addiction;
- eating disorders;
- OCD (Obsessive Compulsive Disorder);
- phobias;
- fear of dying following a diagnosis of terminal illness;
- bereavement;
- anxiety; and
- depression.

In fact, in recent trials, scientists have demonstrated that psilocybin (the active ingredient in magic mushrooms), is a powerful anti-depressant, far more so than traditional anti-depressants. We can use psychedelics in conjunction with "talking therapies" to help people open up and discover deep truths about themselves. Psychedelics also have the effect of instigating profound feelings of love, awe, and connectedness, and the realization that everything is one. This means they help people develop empathy. In short, psychedelics, used correctly and sparingly, are a spiritual tool that can radically alter your perception of yourself and your relationship to the universe, regardless of where you are on your spiritual journey. They open the connection between your conscious mind and your superconscious mind, or higher self, both at the time of taking them and for the longer term.

There's a reason human beings have been using psychedelic substances for millennia. Everything occurring naturally on the Earth is here for a reason—that's the design of our universe. We were always intended to unlock the powers inherent in these plants—respectfully and with purpose. As well as alleviating "negative" symptoms, psychedelics can enhance positive qualities, such as co-operative working and creativity.

Micro-Dosing

Micro-dosing psilocybin has become standard practice in Silicon Valley and other forward-thinking communities. It helps people work together better, solve problems more effectively, and be more creatively productive. The idea of micro-dosing (taking a substance regularly in very small amounts) is that it's "sub-perceptual," so as with CBD oil, you don't get high or "trip." It's a low-key, accessible way to get the benefits of these kinds of compounds.

Micro-dosing can be exceptionally beneficial for someone going through a growth-oriented Dark Night of the Soul. It lifts mood, increases connection, and facilitates deep insight into ourselves and our lives. However, I wouldn't recommend this protocol while going through a spiritual Dark Night. There are a lot of changes happening at system level during this time and the use of psychedelics could interrupt the delicate procedures your team is carrying out. Having said that, micro-dosing can be a useful tool either side of the spiritual Dark Night, especially as it will help your team to deliver messages with increased clarity.

If you decide to explore using psychedelics, it's essential to do so in a safe, legal way, perhaps under formal supervision. If you live in the United States, California has legalized these substances for personal use, and other states are looking to follow. Other countries that allow these types of drugs include Brazil, Canada, The Netherlands, Jamaica, Portugal, and Peru. Many of these countries have organizations that offer psychedelic retreats (vet them and go with someone you trust), or you can apply to join one of many ongoing clinical trials around the World.

Psychedelic Medical Trials

There's little doubt psychedelics, like cannabis, will be licensed for medical use within a few years. Advanced trials around the world are producing astounding results. These new therapies have the potential to be profoundly beneficial to both individuals and society as a whole, particularly in the context of the globe's current mental health crisis. One day the use of psychedelic therapies will be standard medicinal practice.

***

Chapter 8—Spiritual Practice Protocols

The practices listed here are what society today considers to be "spiritual." However, all the protocols in this book are spiritual in one way or another. They promote the balance of mind, body, and spirit, help you connect to the universe and your higher self, and lead you to a happier, more fulfilling, self-actualized life. The farther you proceed along the spiritual awakening path, the more this will become obvious to you, as it is to me now.

Life is spiritual! So, live in a way true to you at soul level, and you're living spiritually. That said, these practices will advance you more quickly (and less painfully) through your Dark Night of the Soul. When you're choosing your preferred protocols to guide you to the other side, prioritize these.

***

Protocol 16: Meditate Daily

As I mentioned in the introduction to Part II of this book, this is the one practice that *above all* will help you build a strong spiritual foundation and speed up your progress through the Dark Night of the Soul. Even if you're not experiencing a Dark Night, meditation is still the cornerstone of all spiritual practice, which is why it's so central to Zen Buddhism. Recall that Zen is the cultural norm in the higher dimensions. As we journey toward global enlightenment, it will become increasingly established on Earth, until it's our way of life too. The good news is, there are many ways to practice meditation, not all of them obvious. For example, walking in nature in silent contemplation is meditative. So is yoga. So are drawing and painting—in fact, all the creative arts are a form of meditation (more on this in Chapter 10). Still, it's crucial that we establish a daily, formal meditation practice to keep us connected and allow clear communication with our team.

Five Minutes Meditation Every Day Can Be Enough

More good news—as little as five minutes of meditation a day will have a significant impact on your overall wellbeing and spiritual progress. I'll show you a super-easy approach anyone can do and that doesn't require experience or equipment. While five minutes a day will get you a good way along, if you're going through the spiritual Dark Night, I encourage you to commit as much time as you can to meditation, at least until you're out the other side. Note that, during the spiritual Dark Night of the Soul, you won't "feel" the usual connection meditation brings, however, you're still integrating in the background.

Once you're through the Dark Night of the Soul, you can dial it down (although it's still important to find time for meditation every day). You won't notice too much if you miss one day, but after missing two, you'll feel your connection fading away. So it's important to get back in the saddle and re-establish your practice should you let it lapse.

Recommended Meditation Technique: Third Eye Meditation.

The meditation practice I recommend to everyone who is still in the process of integrating with their higher self is "third eye" meditation. It will speed things up immeasurably. In fact, it can even trigger the start of your conscious awakening. The best time to meditate is first thing in the morning as soon as you wake up, and the best position in which to meditate is lying down. It really couldn't be any easier.

Exercise: Third Eye Meditation

Lie in bed with your legs straight out and your arms by your side. Close your eyes, relax, and take three deep breaths (this is a signal to the universe that you are going into meditation mode). Then put your awareness in your third eye—the spot just above and between your eyebrows. Visualize a bright light coming from where your third eye is located and keep your focus there. You may find, if you are in a spiritual Dark Night, that it's difficult to visualize. That's OK. Just rest your awareness in your third eye. Now, listen to your breath. You are aiming to achieve a state of conscious awareness, with no chatter from your subconscious or Ego. If you're brand new to meditation, this will take time (perhaps weeks) to achieve. Again, that's OK. It's a process. If thoughts intrude during this practice, as soon as you become conscious that your mind has wandered, just place your awareness back in your third eye.

***

If you can meditate in this way for five minutes twice a day, in the morning and just before you go to bed, I promise you, you'll see a difference very soon. Even if you're practised at meditation but haven't tried this method, give it a whirl. Strengthening your third eye increases clarity of communication with the "other side" and enhances your powers of manifestation.

The Power of "Micro-Meditation"

You can combine the third eye method with a "micro-meditation" practice. Micro-meditation just means snatching a minute here and there throughout your day to meditate. You can do it anytime, anywhere, whenever you have a few minutes to fill, standing, sitting, or lying down:
- waiting for the kettle to boil;
- standing in a queue;
- sitting in a traffic jam; and
- in the shower, for example.

You'll find these snatched moments soon add up.

Meditation is such an important tool for getting through the Dark Night of the Soul, and for general spiritual health, that I encourage you to keep trying different approaches until you find one that works for you. If you prefer a guided meditation, that's fine. Just be aware that it will make it harder to communicate with your team as you'll be focused on the words of the meditation rather than messages coming through.

Meditation is "Sacred"

One excellent reason to commit to a regular meditation practice is that the universe considers meditation "sacred." Only when you're in a formal meditative state can you be sure the communication you're receiving is from your team.

For this reason, you'll always receive honest guidance during meditation (outside of the "judgement" learning phase I spoke of earlier). Or, if your team can't provide certain information for any reason, they'll let you know, for example, the time might not be right.

Misinformation

Outside of meditation, if you're clairaudient and your communication channel is open, others might try to misdirect you. Perhaps they're on the "opposing team" and trying to prevent you succeeding in your plan. This is especially likely if you're a higher evolved soul with an important mission. Remember, we're playing the Game of Life. The farther you progress through your awakening, the more you'll be able to differentiate between accurate information and messages intended to mislead. Setting aside prescribed time for a one-on-one, uninterrupted chat with your higher self during meditation means you can be sure you're receiving bona fide guidance when you need it.

> *Exercise: Establish a Daily Meditation Routine*
>
> *Set your alarm for ten minutes earlier each morning and use this extra time for a third eye meditation.*

***

Protocol 17: Try Self-Hypnosis

Meditation is a technique for getting into a low-level trance. Trance is the state whereby your brain produces more theta waves and fewer alpha and beta waves. Theta waves are the "frequency" of the higher dimensions and that's why you experience enhanced intuition or outright communication from your team during meditation sessions. You're "tuning in." Don't worry if you haven't experienced this yet. Keep going with your practice and you soon will.

There are other safe and simple ways to get into a trance. One of these is self-hypnosis. Those seeking to re-program their subconscious so they can stop drinking, smoking, or over-eating (for example), sometimes employ self-hypnosis. But you can also use it as a way to connect to your higher self and guides.

To get through the Dark Night of the Soul, anything that helps you connect is good because it means you're continuing to integrate in parallel. You might not feel it, but you are. And if you use self-hypnosis outside of the spiritual Dark Night to connect with your higher self, it can result in some startling revelations. This is because it's a deeper level of trance than most of us can achieve in meditation. It takes your subconscious out of the equation so you can enjoy virtually unfettered access to the higher echelons. As an example, I used self-hypnosis to discover the name of my soul (Persephone) and to meet my higher self (Sophia) for the first time. I have also used this protocol to access past life memories. It's a great tool to unlock specific information.

If you want to try self-hypnosis for spiritual connection, you'll find many suitable videos on YouTube. Just listen through headphones while lying in a comfortable position somewhere you won't be disturbed. My team also pointed me towards a book called "Instant Self-Hypnosis: How to Hypnotize Yourself with Your Eyes Open[x]," by Forbes Robbins Blair, which I can recommend.

Exercise: Try Self-Hypnosis.

Put aside an hour for a self-hypnosis session. Decide on your intention—what do you want to learn, or who do you want to meet? Find a suitable video on YouTube, one you feel drawn to. Before you start your self-hypnosis session, state your intention clearly and ask your guides to provide the answers you're looking for.

***

Protocol 18: Teach Yourself to Lucid Dream

Lucid dreaming is something my team encouraged me to do right at the beginning of my spiritual awakening journey. Lucid dreaming means knowing you're in a dream at the time you are dreaming. While we dream, we visit other dimensions. This makes it easier for our teams and other entities to interact with us, which is why we receive messages so often while we are asleep. If you can control your dream state via lucid dreaming, it becomes a potent exploratory tool.

As with self-hypnosis, you can set the intention before you fall asleep that you want to receive specific information in your dreams that night. If you're practicing lucid dreaming it's easier for you to seek and receive this while in dream state, otherwise, as we all know, dreams have a tendency to meander off. My team told me that, if we perform spiritual protocols within a dream, such as meditation or yoga, they have an exponential impact. This means you'll speed up integration with your higher self. The same is true of manifestation techniques. If conducted within a lucid dream, they're far more potent.

When I was a teenager, I taught myself to lucid dream and had some extremely interesting experiences, without knowing at that age to relate them to spirituality. However, I stopped when I was sixteen. I found myself, terrified, floating above my sleeping body, connected by a silver cord, about to whoosh out the window! I wonder what would have happened if I'd let myself go, or continued my lucid dreaming practice into adulthood. Much later, after my conscious awakening, my team asked me to relearn to lucid dream and I used the technique to meet one of my primary guides (Om). It was a life-changing experience. It's no exaggeration to say that lucid dreaming is one of the most potent tools available to us in our earthly incarnations.

Lucid Dreaming During a Dark Night of the Soul

If you're in a growth-oriented Dark Night of the Soul, lucid dreaming can help you uncover the underlying causes and the truths about why you're feeling like you are. In this respect, it's a bit like the psychedelic therapies I discussed in Protocol 15. If you're in a spiritual

Dark Night, lucid dreaming provides you with an opportunity to connect with your team, which is difficult to do during this stage of awakening. This protocol can benefit everyone, whatever their stage of spiritual development, so it's worth adding to your repertoire of techniques. It takes practice, but if you're a higher evolved soul (which you probably are if you're reading this book), you'll discover you're a natural.

Charlie Morley

The modern expert in lucid dreaming techniques is Charlie Morley. He has published several books and has a YouTube channel. I used one of his books to relearn how to lucid dream, so I can recommend him. Here's a link to Charlie's website: https://www.charliemorley.com/[xi].

> *Exercise: Research Lucid Dreaming*
>
> *Put some time aside to look at Charlie Morley's website or YouTube channel and decide if you are ready to explore this protocol now.*

***

Protocol 19: Use Energy Clearing Exercises

I use energy clearing exercises from time to time to remove blockages from my system and keep things flowing. If you're going through a Dark Night of the Soul, I suggest you perform an energy clearing protocol at least every other day. Here's a simple routine you can use:

> *Exercise: Perform an Energy Clearing Ritual*
>
> *Step 1:*

Lie down in a comfortable position, just as you would to meditate.

Step 2:

Meditate briefly to clear your mind—just a couple of minutes should do.

Step 3:

State out loud or clearly in your mind your intention to clear any energy blockages in your system.

Step 4:

Visualize a bright light entering your body through your crown chakra at the top of your head. The light can be any color you choose. See this light descending and whooshing through your body, exiting through your feet. Continue this visualization while performing Step 5 below.

Step 5:

Repeat the following affirmation three times, out loud or in your mind: "My energy centers are completely unblocked."

***

If you're in a spiritual Dark Night of the Soul you may find the above exercise tough going as it requires visualization and the spiritual Dark Night inhibits this ability. However, it will still have positive benefits, even if you can't conjure up a clear image. I perform an energy clearing ritual every week or so (or when I sense an imbalance in my system) so it's worth including in your ongoing spiritual routine, to maintain chakra health. The farther through your awakening you progress, the more you'll become sensitive to energetic blockages and know when to take remedial action. Outside of a Dark Night of the Soul, typical signs of an energy imbalance or blockage are:

- low mood or lethargy;
- irritability;
- lack of patience;
- low level anxiety;
- niggling physical issues, such as headaches or constipation;
- losing contact with your team or feeling disconnected.

Using an Energy Healer

During my second spiritual Dark Night of the Soul, I engaged the services of an energy healer. He was based in the U.S. and performed the exercise over Zoom, so a practitioner can do it from a distance. It wasn't cheap, but I noticed an immediate effect. If you feel you're especially sluggish, you might want to do the same.

***

Protocol 20: Practice Grounding

Grounding is an important practice for everyone, whether or not they consider themselves "spiritual." In fact, the UK's National Health Service recommends it to help with a whole host of "mental" conditions, especially anxiety. Grounding is a form of meditation, but one that focuses on reassuring the physical part of the system (the body and subconscious), so they reduce the output of negative emotions. As well as calming your body, grounding allows your mind to ascend to the higher dimensions more freely—remember, a happy body is more comfortable about letting you soar off.

If you're not familiar with grounding, it does what it says on the tin. You're reconnecting to the ground, or earth.

Exercise: Ground Yourself

An easy way to ground yourself is to stand in bare feet (outdoors on the grass or soil is ideal). Close your eyes. Visualize roots growing from the soles of your feet down into the earth. If you don't have easy access to private outdoor space or it's the middle of winter, you can just do this exercise standing or sitting in a chair in the living room. In this practice, it's important your feet are flat on the floor, so it's different to other forms of meditation that are best performed lying down. But in every other respect, it's the same protocol as third eye meditation, you are just putting your awareness in the soles of your feet rather than your third eye.

***

Other Methods of Grounding

You can calm the physical part of your system in other ways. Here's a few tips:

- eat a small amount of high quality sugar, such as manuka honey;
- take a shower or bath;
- make sure your body is comfortably warm;
- take a few long, deep breaths;
- go for a walk in nature;
- stand in the sunshine with your face upturned.

***

Protocol 21: Practice Gratitude

Practicing gratitude is becoming increasingly common. This is a splendid development, both for individuals and the collective consciousness. Practicing gratitude means you take time each day to express your thanks for the good things in your life. You can be thankful for something small, like a good cup of coffee, or something big, like your health and talents.

Gratitudes put you in a positive frame of mind, which means you'll manifest positive things. This is helpful when you're going through an episode of the Dark Night of the Soul. During the Dark Night you'll feel at odds with the world. You're unlikely to manifest the good stuff and increasingly likely to manifest the bad (although in a spiritual Dark Night, your team will protect you from this to some degree). If you can incorporate a gratitude practice into your daily routine, it will help keep you at least on a neutral footing.

In terms of any Dark Night of the Soul, more gratitude is better, so try to find quiet moments throughout the day to perform a quick ritual. It doesn't need to take long. Gratitudes work best if you can feel grateful while you're saying them, but if you're struggling with that, the words alone will still have a positive impact. Below I provide examples of gratitude statements specifically for the spiritual Dark Night of the Soul. It's best to state them out loud, I find looking in a mirror helps too.

Exercise: Perform a Gratitude Ritual for the Spiritual Dark Night of the Soul

Stand in front of a mirror and repeat the following phrases:

- *Thank you for the love you give me;*

- *Thank you for this experience;*
- *Thank you for my lessons;*
- *Thank you for choosing me to be part of this important project;*
- *Thank you for giving me the chance to prove myself.*

If you're experiencing a growth-oriented Dark Night, then try these:

Exercise: Perform a Gratitude Ritual for the Growth-Oriented Dark Night of the Soul

Stand in front of a mirror and repeat the following phrases:

- *Thank you for the light at the end of the tunnel;*
- *Thank you for the strength to get through this experience;*
- *Thank you for giving me the impetus I need to change my life;*
- *Thank you for the good things I know are waiting for me in my future.*

***

Hand on heart, during the Dark Night of the Soul, I didn't always feel grateful! But I felt a mood boost after I had completed a gratitude ritual, so it became an important part of my routine. There are many excellent guided gratitude meditations on YouTube if you choose to explore further.

Showing Gratitude to Your Team

Whether or not you're going through a Dark Night, it's nice to say, "Thank you" to your team. They do an enormous amount for us, whether we're aware of it or not. You may not know it, but there are millions of souls in the universe who are rooting for you and following your progress. This, in a sense, is your wider team. Thanking them for their support deepens those bonds and creates a sense of wellbeing on both sides. I use a little catechism each morning, just before I ask the universe for help. Here are the exact words I use:

Exercise: Say Thank You to Your Team.

After meditation and before "prayer" (see Protocol 23) repeat these words, out loud or clearly in your mind:

- *Thank you for your faith in me;*
- *Thank you for your love of me;*
- *Thank you for all the help you have given me in the past;*
- *Thank you for the help you are giving me today;*
- *Thank you for the help I know you will give me in the future.*

***

Showing Gratitude to Your Body

Another thing we rarely think to do is to say "Thank you" to our body, but it's an important part of our overall system and works hard for us, always trying to do the right thing. Getting into the habit of thanking it gives it reassurance and helps to open up dialogue between the subconscious mind (body) and conscious mind (soul). Because, believe it or not, our bodies are listening to us.

If you can get used to thanking your physical being for its service and giving it clear direction as to what you want, you will find this is an excellent foundation for self-healing and other improvements, such as weight loss or freeing yourself from addiction.

***

Protocol 22: Affirmations and Visualizations

Affirmations and visualizations are crucial tools in spiritual practice and, used correctly, can speed your passage through the Dark Night of the Soul. When affirming, we state something we want to have happen, or something we want to become. For maximum effectiveness, frame affirmations in the present tense, as if they have already happened. Below are some examples of affirmations:

- I am happy, healthy, and whole;
- I am at my ideal weight;
- I am with my soulmate;
- I never have to worry about money;
- I excel at my career.

You can see from this list that you can frame whatever you want for yourself as an affirmation.

How to Use Affirmations

The best time to perform your affirmation ritual is straight after meditation, in the morning. There are a few tricks you can use to get the most out of your affirmation practice.

1. Combine Written and Spoken Affirmations

Write down a list of no more than five or six short and simple affirmations, on your phone or a piece of paper, somewhere you can easily access at any time. Each morning, read this list. These are the affirmations you will also use in your spoken ritual, employing the techniques below.

2. *Always Couple an Affirmation with a Visualization*

A visualization is a picture in your mind that represents the words you are saying. Pick a powerful, symbolic image you can maintain in your mind with little effort. This engages your imagination—your primary tool of manifestation.

3. *Make Your First Affirmation Manifestation-Enhancing*

The first affirmation of your ritual should always relate to enhancing your manifestation abilities. I use:

"I am a powerful manifester. Everything I desire, I create."

Few people are aware of this brilliant hack, but it's super-powerful. Basically, you're manifesting yourself as a powerful manifester! If you remember to do this, your following affirmations will carry more weight.

4. *Say Each Affirmation Three Times*

There's a good reason for this—it signals to the universe you are setting an intention. When you think about it, it's logical. If you say something once, it could just be part of a conversation. If you say something twice, you might just be adding emphasis. But if you say something three times, it's intentional. Think of it as a secret code you share with the universe.

5. *Feel What You're Saying*

As with a gratitude practice, affirmations work best if you can "feel" what you're saying. For example, if you're using the affirmation, "I never have to worry about money," summoning up the feeling of being light and anxiety-free will amplify your intention. This can take a little practice but it's possible (actors do it all the time).

6. Learn to Compartmentalize

Compartmentalization is an important part of using affirmations successfully. It just means being able to store thoughts in a distant part of your mind so you're not accessing them continually. If we yearn for something or we're anxious about it, we keep turning it over in our minds, worrying. This inhibits its manifestation. For example, every time you ask, "Will my money concerns disappear?" or "When is the money coming?" you have diluted the power of your original affirmative statement: "I never have to worry about money." It's self-defeating. Train yourself to put your affirmations aside once you've performed your morning ritual, and interrupt any thought patterns throughout the day, questioning whether the affirmation will manifest.

7. Believe Your Affirmations Will Come True

It will help you in your affirmation practice if you can build belief. There's a neat trick you can use to help with this. Start off with a couple of small, short-term affirmations you could reasonably expect to manifest in a month or less. Practice your affirmation ritual conscientiously. As long as you aren't asking for things that take you a long way from your true path, they will almost certainly happen. Once you have evidence that you can manifest things in this way, it will be easier to believe that the big things are coming down the track. It also helps to sign off your affirmation ritual with a positive statement such as, "I now release all anxiety and fear related to these affirmations and trust in my team and the universe to deliver them as they see fit."

8. *Be Patient*

The larger the thing you ask for is, the longer it will take to arrive. Why? Because the universe has more to arrange. Remember, we inhabit a dense, physical plane where it takes more time for things to manifest than in the higher dimensions. For enormous things, you can expect to wait a few years (unless it was in your pre-incarnation plan and is hiding just around the corner). Don't give up hope. Keep asking and believing the universe will deliver.

Exercise: Supercharge Your Affirmation Practice.

Write down a small number of things you wish to manifest. Keep them simple and in the present tense. Organise the list according to the time you think it will take to manifest each one—the quickest ones first. Build time into your morning meditation routine to start using these affirmations, employing the tips outlined above.

There's one more thing you can do to boost the power of your affirmations and speed up manifestation. It's "prayer." My team told me early on in my awakening that, "Affirmations, visualizations, and prayer are the holy trinity of manifestation." If we use all three in conjunction, this is the most powerful manifestation protocol we can employ. I talk about prayer, or asking the universe for help, in the next protocol.

***

Protocol 23: Pray/Ask the Universe for Help

People can get uncomfortable around the word "prayer" but there's no need. Whatever your religious beliefs, all it means is asking for help. Sophia tells me she wishes more people would ask for help. This is because the rules of the Game of Life prohibit our teams from doing whatever they want—the request for assistance needs to come from us (remember, we're the CEOs of our own lives).

Those millions of souls in the wider universe, who are following your progress and wishing you well, all have the power to manifest on your behalf—but only if you ask them to. When you "pray," they're listening. It's their good wishes and powers of manifestation, added to your own, that help you realize your dreams. I ask the universe for help immediately following my affirmations ritual and also use prayer as a standalone practice.

Exercise: Ask for Help

Step 1:

Perform your affirmation ritual as described in Protocol 22 above.

Step 2:

Use the catechism described in Protocol 21 as an introduction to your "prayer":

- *Thank you for your faith in me;*
- *Thank you for your love of me;*
- *Thank you for all the help you have given me in the past;*
- *Thank you for the help you are giving me today;*
- *Thank you for the help I know you will give me in the future.*
- *I am asking for your help now....*

Step 3:

State clearly what you want help with. Typically this will be the same as your list of affirmations, in fact, you can "short-cut" your prayer by simply asking for help manifesting these. I also include requests on behalf of other people, providing things such as good health, financial luck, and spiritual protection.

***

Asking For Help During the Dark Night of the Soul

The Dark Night of the Soul is exactly the time to request support and guidance. You can ask the universe to give you strength to get through to the other side and speed up your integration with your higher self. As with all protocols, the power of a prayer starts to drop off after twenty four hours, so it helps to repeat your request daily.

***

Protocol 24: Talk to Your Team Even If You Feel They're Not Listening

One of the hardest things for me going into the spiritual Dark Night of the Soul was the almost total loss of communication with my team. Over the previous six months, I had got to know an entire cast of characters who, even though I'd only just met them in this incarnation, had been there all my life and knew me intimately. Because you and your team are old friends, when you make contact with them from your earthly vantage point, it feels like coming home. You have truly "found your tribe." They become your confidantes, your advisors, and your cheerleaders. So, for them to not be there suddenly—or rather, for you to be unable to perceive them any longer—well, you feel as though the universe has pulled the rug out from under your feet.

The fact is, your guides are still there, and they're missing you too. Speaking to them now and again comforts both them and you. Tell them you love them, tell them you're thankful for everything they've done to bring you this far, and tell them you're looking forward to being with them again soon. This creates a sense of wellbeing for both you and them.

***

Protocol 25: Connect with Other People

This may not feel like a spiritual practice protocol but it is. In our universe, everything exerts energy on everything else. When we spend time with other people, especially those who care about us, we receive a positive energy charge. Connecting with others helps us "power up." The challenge with the Dark Night of the Soul is that we turn inward and seek solitude. The constriction of our chakras decreases our desire to spend time with people.

While solitude can be beneficial, it's never healthy to cut ourselves off completely from others. We are "pack" creatures, at both human and soul level, and need the energy that connection brings. You know from experience how much better you feel after talking about your problems to someone sympathetic. There's no time at which this is more crucial than during an episode of the Dark Night. I'm not suggesting you go out partying if you don't feel up to it. But if you have a good friend you can speak to or, even better, spend time with, it will give you a boost that's difficult to get in any other way. (Why not go for an energizing walk in nature together?) If you can't deal with a face to face, spend some quality time on social media. This is still a form of connection.

Exercise: Reach Out

Make a list of people you know are sympathetic and supportive. If there's one you feel particularly drawn to, reach out to them and suggest catching up in whatever way is most comfortable to you—in person, on Zoom, or with a phone call. It's OK to tell them you're having a tough time and you'd like to talk. Don't shy away from speaking about the Dark Night of the Soul, my experience tells me people are more receptive than we anticipate.

***

Chapter 9—Self-Development Protocols

All self-development is "spiritual" and spiritual growth is self-development. Once you accept the idea that we're all immortal souls who incarnate time after time into human lives, primarily to learn, this becomes obvious. Working to become the "best version" of ourselves in a given lifetime, not only helps us as individuals, but also benefits the entire community of souls on a universal scale. It does this in two ways:

- first, the collective consciousness absorbs the things we learn. That means that not only do we progress ourselves, but the entire group moves forward;

- second, improving your state of mind—feeling happy—raises the collective vibration. Again, everyone benefits.

It may feel that during the Dark Night of the Soul is not the best time to embark on self-development, but if you're experiencing a growth-oriented Dark Night, it's exactly what you need to do. Something sub-optimal in your life or behavior has caused you to spiral downward. Self-development is a crucial remedy, perhaps the only remedy. Even in a spiritual Dark Night, where you're likely to be more advanced in your self-development (otherwise your team wouldn't have initiated your conscious spiritual awakening), there are probably a few things that need ironing out. Thinking about these can give you a renewed sense of purpose and a plan to move forward, even if you're not ready to put it into action quite yet. Because we're all spiritual beings and self-development is a spiritual act, every one of us can benefit from the protocols I provide below. The good news is that self-development, while hard, has the power to be completely transformative. It can literally change your life.

***

Protocol 26: Keep a Diary or Blog

Keeping a diary or writing a blog is a great way to start your inner work. It generates self-awareness, which is crucial to self-improvement and spiritual awakening. Regular, honest documenting of our actions, thoughts, and emotions helps us see patterns in our lives and psyche. These can create useful "Aha!" moments. Think about it. How can you invest in your development if you don't know what you need to work on? Keeping a journal can illuminate your path. During the Dark Night of the Soul, journaling can help you see the correlation between your actions and your mood. You can identify (and eliminate) the behaviors or situations that cause you to dip, and do more of the things that give you a lift.

Journaling is a lot like cognitive behavioral therapy, or "CBT," which is focused on building self-awareness. Writing things down is a great way to excise them from your system and release pent-up emotions. Sometimes we don't know how we feel until we explore in this way, and the revelations that result can be truly eye-opening. Remember too, at a later stage in life, you may want to remember or share details of your experiences, to help others overcome their own adversities. As a higher evolved soul, part of your purpose is to teach. Things can get fuzzy from a distance, so having a diary or blog to refer to can be useful.

Exercise: Start a Journal

Buy a diary or choose a journaling app. Put aside time at the end of each day to note what happened, what you did, and your resulting feelings. Re-read earlier journal entries frequently and look for patterns which indicate where you need to make changes in your circumstances or behavior.

***

Protocol 27: Research

When you're going through a Dark Night of the Soul and are likely to have long periods of inactivity, it's the perfect time for research. Knowledge is power. What you research is up to you and will depend on your situation. For example, if you're in a growth-oriented Dark Night, it will be helpful to read up on the circumstances that brought you here and your specific symptoms. If you're going through a spiritual Dark Night, you can immerse yourself in metaphysical texts. Anything concerning Zen philosophy and practices will be helpful too. Once you're fully integrated and transcended, you'll discover you're naturally living in a "Zen" way.

As much as the Dark Night allows them to, your team will lead you to the texts you need. It's easy for your guides to manipulate digital data, so conducting your research on the internet will give them a greater opportunity to put the right information in front of you. (This is true whether or not you're going through the Dark Night.) Choose well-researched, robust content by experts, so you can be confident you're receiving the right guidance. Learning more about yourself and the universe we inhabit will give you confidence that you can improve yourself and your situation, and that there's something bigger out there you can connect with. Pieces of the puzzle will start to drop into place.

***

Protocol 28: Do Your Inner Work

No-one can advance spiritually without doing inner work. As human beings, we cannot avoid accruing trauma and negative thought patterns and behaviors—it's part of the human condition.

By "doing inner work" I mean we untangle these issues. Deep inner work is essential to creating a stable mental and emotional platform so you can continue along your spiritual path. This is especially true if you're going through a growth-oriented Dark Night of the Soul. Without addressing the underlying causes of your spiritual depression, it will be difficult to move forward or avoid a relapse.

It would require an entire book (perhaps several), to describe all the various ways we self-sabotage in our human incarnations, but in summary, the majority of issues we experience fall into a few broad areas. These are:

- too-high or too-low self-esteem;
- depressive disorders;
- anxiety;
- Obsessive Compulsive Disorder;
- Post-Traumatic Stress Disorder;
- crippling feelings of guilt or shame;
- fear;
- phobias;
- lack of empathy;
- over-emotionality;
- anger-management issues;
- lack of resilience;
- self-sabotaging behaviors;
- addiction.

These conditions are often interlinked, so if you have one, you may have several. There are also more deeply rooted psychiatric conditions such as bi-polar disorder, schizophrenia, sociopathy, psychopathy, narcissism, and borderline personality disorder. If you suspect you have one of these conditions, consult a professional. These are not the issues I'm talking about here.

The good news is, as you work on one area of self-development, others will start to naturally resolve. In other words, inner work gets easier as you continue. That's not to say it's a walk in the park. It requires dissolving patterns of thought and behavior that have become part of you and may have persisted for a long time. Inner work is especially hard because it requires you to look yourself in the face and scrutinize your own actions, which nobody enjoys doing.

The Particular Challenge of Low Self-Esteem

Inner work is especially difficult if you suffer from low self-esteem, as many higher evolved souls do in their human forms. Low self-esteem comes about because of the difficult events we often experience in our early lives, such as neglect and abuse. (Recall that these trials and tribulations were planned prior to our incarnation—they are designed to anchor us to the physical and help us learn.) Self-esteem gives rise to self-limiting behaviors—we don't believe we're worthy or capable, and this can prevent us from pursuing inner work. If you know or suspect you suffer from low self-esteem, then tackle this development need first.

How to Know Where to Focus Inner Work

One pre-requisite of undertaking inner work is that you have to know what it is you need to "fix." When you are looking from the inside out, this can be difficult, but I encourage you to persevere and try to put a name to your "issues." You can use your journal to identify patterns

(Protocol 26) and research your "symptoms", both of these will help shine a light.

I have also found that, when we start asking ourselves searching question about the events in our lives and the impact they've had on us, the universe often puts people in our way who have had uncannily similar experiences. Typically they'll be further along the path of inner work than we are ourselves. It's a classic case of, "When the pupil is ready, the teacher will come". Don't be shy of discussing your own journey with these people, they will help you.

You also have the option of seeking professional support. I talk about this in Protocols 29 and 30.

Inner Work During the Dark Night of the Soul

You may decide that the Dark Night of the Soul isn't the right time to embark on inner work. If you're going through a spiritual Dark Night, this might be the case, for two reasons:

- first, to have come so far in your spiritual journey, you have already resolved a lot of your "human" issues. Whatever is left is more about tying up the final details;

- second, because the universe has constricted all of your chakras to a significant degree, you have little energy or ability to focus.

If this is the case, feel free to park any inner work until later in your journey. Just keep in mind that there are likely to be things you need to deal with once you feel stronger.

In a growth-oriented Dark Night, however, inner work is of paramount importance, so I encourage you to take steps, however tentative, toward getting the work done. It's important during any sort of self-exploration that you're kind to yourself and forgive yourself for anything you did in the past you're not proud of. In this way, you'll move forward.

Inner Work During Other Stages of the Spiritual Journey

If you're not experiencing a Dark Night of the Soul but you're interested in spiritual development, inner work is a must. It builds the stable platform you need for conscious awakening. If you're aware you have things you need to work on, and you want to progress spiritually, then make inner work a priority.

***

Protocol 29: Consider Therapy

If you feel you need extra support for your inner work, a therapist can help you, often in just a few sessions. A good therapist is invaluable because they can:

- provide an objective point of view;
- give you emotional support as you go through the process;
- provide a benchmark of "normality;"
- put labels on your "condition" to help you with understanding and research;
- reassure you that everything is fixable, or at least manageable.

A therapist doesn't have to cost a fortune—there are reasonably priced services available online these days. If you invest in the process and do the necessary work, you will find the tools to continue moving forward on your own. The money I spent on therapy is the best investment I ever made. Without it, I wouldn't be where I am today. So, wherever you are on your spiritual journey, if you battle underlying issues, this is an avenue worth exploring. The stigma associated with seeking therapy long ago evaporated, so please don't feel ashamed. Go for it.

***

Protocol 30: Find a Coach or Teacher

I'm sure you've heard the phrase, "When the student is ready the teacher will appear", in fact, I've used it in this book. Speaking personally, this has been the case in my life. I feel lucky to have learned from some of the most accomplished people in their fields. You can get a lot farther, faster, by leveraging other people's experience and knowledge. You don't have to reinvent the wheel.

You may not need to embark on a course of therapy; perhaps you could just do with some steering. Signing up with a coach or teacher, even just for a short while, can be beneficial. They don't even need to be a formal coach. Perhaps you know someone who has solved the problem you're struggling with. Why not reach out to them and ask how they did it? This is how things work in the higher dimensions—souls help other souls and learn from each other all the time. It's our primary instinct and the way we designed our society. With higher evolved souls (especially ones who have completed at least some of their inner work), this desire to help flows through into their earthly incarnation. So don't be shy or embarrassed about asking someone for guidance, they'll almost certainly be happy to help.

***

Protocol 31: Get Rid of Bad Habits

Here we're talking about patterns of behavior that are detrimental to your well-being, and hold back your personal development. Shedding bad habits is vital for progression on the awakening journey.

Bad habits can take lots of forms. Yes, there are the ones we're all familiar with, such as smoking or drinking, but consider these, too:

- being glued to your smartphone;
- watching too much tv;
- procrastination;
- failing to speak your mind;
- allowing others to pressure or bully you;
- spending time with people you dislike or who are bad for you;
- over-spending;
- being lax in your spiritual routine;
- allowing yourself to do sloppy work;
- letting people down, or shirking your commitments.

These are all examples of bad habits and self-limiting behaviors that prevent us from moving forward. To break a bad habit, the first step is, as always, awareness.

We All Have Bad Habits

If you feel you have nothing you need to improve on, I have disappointing news for you—you do. Perhaps you're 90 percent there, but I guarantee, you're not at 100 percent. Virtually no one is. While there are a few notable cases in history—the Buddha and the Prophet Muhammad spring to mind—it's not always the way with more recent spiritual leaders. For example, Gandhi indulged in unusual sexual practices[xii] and Mother Teresa's life was mired in numerous controversies towards the end[xiii]. Even Jesus had occasional outbursts of anger[xiv]. I give these examples, not to undermine these distinguished figures, but to illustrate that it's difficult to shed every one of our bad habits in full.

If you're at peace with your actions and aware that your beneficial behaviors far outweigh the bad, you're in a good place. You can decide for yourself if you wish to "shoot for the moon" or not. Choosing to work on your behavior is your prerogative, just decide consciously. And remember, self-development = spiritual development. We are souls who came here to learn. So, if you want to move forward spiritually, this is the kind of self-examination and commitment to improvement you'll have to make.

How To Become Aware of Bad Habits

If you're not sure if you have bad habits you need to break, or you need help spotting them, ask people you trust for feedback. If they identify negative behaviors, ask them to give you concrete examples, so you can be sure they're coming from an objective viewpoint.

Step back and examine the evidence from a distance. Do they have a point? Where do you need to focus? Asking for this kind of feedback is uncomfortable, but if you approach people you know care about you and want to see you succeed, understand they are trying to help. If you want to be the best version of yourself you can possibly be, learning to take other people's comments on board is essential. And of course, the people closest to us tend to know us better than we do ourselves, at least until we've transcended.

This technique is often used as part of performance reviews in big business—it's called "360-degree feedback." One of the nice things about this process is that you also receive positive comments that both help you understand more about yourself and contribute to greater self-esteem.

If you're really not comfortable asking others for opinions, conduct a thorough, honest examination of your behaviors yourself. Think back to times when you know you didn't behave at your best. Can you spot the pattern? What's the root cause of your behavior? Or, if you're not getting closer to your goals, sit down and scrutinize your situation. What's blocking you? Are you self-sabotaging?

How to Break Bad Habits

To be able to break bad habits, it's important not to get despondent. In particular, don't let yourself fall prey to guilt and shame. These negative emotions will only hold you back. Remember, by committing to self-improvement, you're already streets ahead of the vast majority of people. You're doing something positive—good for you.

Once you're aware of the areas you need to work on, prioritize them. Which behavior is holding you back the most? Work on that one first. Draw up an action plan. Knowing the specific steps you're going to take is key to success. Your goal is to replace a detrimental behavior with a beneficial behavior, for example:

- replace alcoholic drinks with soft drinks;
- chew gum instead of smoking;
- read a book instead of watching Netflix.

Research techniques and ask for advice, remember, the right teacher will appear for you.

We Are All Re-Programmable

The mind is inordinately flexible. It's an evolving, constantly changing entity, shaped by your thoughts and behaviors. Adopting good habits forges new paths and creates patterns which soon become your norm. I'm sure you know people who have dug deep and made vast changes, to the extent that they're no longer recognizable as the person they once were. If they can do it, you can do it.

Working With a Mentor

If you'd like a little extra support while you're trying to break bad habits, the help of a mentor can be invaluable—as long as you're transparent about what you need to improve and share your progress openly with them. A good mentor is non-judgmental and invested in your success, so can make an enormous difference. Often they're someone you know but who is slightly removed from you—such as a colleague, or friend of a friend.

It's important to pick someone who has some mentoring and/or coaching experience, and to respect their time. A mentor will typically spend half an hour with you every one or two weeks, to check on progress and offer guidance. It's usually fine to message them from time to time if you need extra support or advice, but check with them first. If you agree to the boundaries up front, mentoring arrangements can be beneficial to both parties and can lead to deep, long-lasting friendships.

Exercise: Identify Your Bad Habits

Ask your closest friend or partner, someone who knows you well and whom you trust, to give you some honest feedback. Pick someone who has got their own bad habits and behaviors under control. What have they observed in you that they think you could improve? A good way to phrase the question is, "What is the one thing I could change which would help me be a better, more successful person?". Remember, these people have your best interests at heart and will speak truthfully to you.

***

Protocol 32: Carry Out a Life Audit

Whichever type of Dark Night of the Soul you're in, you need to assess your life and think about any changes you should make. Outside of the Dark Night, it's still helpful to check in occasionally. I do this every New Year's Eve and also if I become aware that I'm unhappy. Remember, as you change (spiritual awakening is transformative, you *will* change), so will your needs and desires. A good time to undertake a " life audit" is once you're a little way down the track with self-development.

The Growth-Oriented Dark Night of the Soul—Life Audit

During a growth-oriented Dark Night, more than any other time, you need to conduct a life audit. Something is making you unhappy. The question is, what? You can't do anything about it if you can't pinpoint the causes. I explain how to do this later in this section.

The Spiritual Dark Night of the Soul—Life Audit

Around the time of a spiritual Dark Night, the universe will start to encourage you to "release what doesn't serve you" (another Zen precept). Again, this necessitates a life audit. In addition, you'll have started to intuit your purpose in this lifetime. Often we need to switch paths to be able to fulfil our missions. Analysing where we are today, versus where we want to get to, allows us to create a plan so we can make the necessary changes.

My own life audit, conducted just after I exited the spiritual Dark Night, led me to leave a career and a marriage, kick a twenty-five-year alcohol addiction, lose thirty pounds in weight, and move to a different country. Your own may not lead to anything as dramatic as that, but be aware that it could. Be receptive to what your instincts are telling you. Don't discount your options because "logic," your loved ones, or society tells you you're "crazy," or it's not possible. Anything is possible. But unless you get clear on what you want for yourself, it's unlikely to happen. The lengthy periods of inert time that accompany a Dark Night of the Soul (whichever type it is) present the perfect opportunity to dissect your life and work out which areas need to improve. This can be a gentle process—in fact, it's good to spend a lot of time mulling over things, as long as you're moving forward in your understanding of yourself and your needs.

How to Conduct a Life Audit

A good place to start is with "absolute truths." When you search deep in your soul, what *must* be true for you to be happy? My own absolute truths were these:

- "A life without painting, for me, is not a life worth living,"
- "I'm unhappy in my marriage and something needs to change,"
- "It's vital for me to live away from the city and close to nature,"
- "I want to contribute something useful to the world,"
- "It's important to me to live in a simpler, less materialistic way,"
- "I need to live in a country with lots of sun."

Digging deep to understand these facts about myself and my circumstances helped me develop the blueprint for how I live now. After gaining this understanding, it was easy to identify the changes I needed to make. It took me another two years to implement them—change doesn't have to happen overnight—but I knew I would get to where I needed to be, whatever it took.

Exercise: Discover Your Absolute Truths

It can be beneficial to perform a short third eye meditation before doing this exercise. Also, ask your team to help you uncover your truths. Take a piece of paper and a pen. Explore each significant area of your life in turn: family, health, career, living situation, finances etc. Score your happiness level out of ten in each area. Write these scores down. Starting with the area which scored the lowest, examine it. What about it is making you unhappy? What changes could you make, small, medium, and large, which would improve it? Continue until you have finished the list. (You may want to complete this exercise over several sessions.)

***

Protocol 33: Make a Plan

Once you know what needs to change, it's time to make a plan. If you're in a spiritual Dark Night of the Soul, you may want to wait until you've navigated your way out, when you'll have more energy and drive. However, you may find that making a plan when you're in the Dark Night comforts you. There's no right or wrong here. Trust your instincts and do what feels best for you.

If you're in a growth-oriented Dark Night, making a plan could be just what you need to help pull you out of your slump. It doesn't have to be big or comprehensive, it just needs to signpost your next few actions (remember, we work in an "agile" way—taking things bit by bit). If you can just move a few steps forward, it will surprise you how quickly things can improve. I'm a firm believer that "doing *something* is better than doing nothing." Even if you're not sure where you want to end up, taking some action, however small, will help you decide if you have chosen the right direction. Then you can build on those first steps.

Let Your Team Help with Your Plan

As I mentioned, another reason to make a plan is so your team can help you. If they know the direction you're heading, they can clear the way. If you combine making a plan with asking the universe to help, they can do even more.

You can also ask your team to help design your plan. This is helpful because 1) they know what you intended before you incarnated, and 2) they know what opportunities are out there waiting for you. If you're already at the point where you're receiving clear, verbal communication when you meditate, then set aside time for a specific meditation session to discuss the options that are open to you. It's important you state your goals clearly, these must come from you and you alone. However, your team will give you advice on how to achieve them.

If you don't yet have clarity of communication with your team, then there are other ways you can get their input. Asking for signs, using divination tools (such as tarot cards), and following your intuition, are all good approaches. You still need to state your goals clearly, then be alert for signals in the following forty-eight hours. Often you will find these come digitally, ads pointing you towards books and articles with the information you need, for example.

***

Protocol 34: Find Your Purpose

One guaranteed outcome of completing the spiritual awakening journey is that you'll "find your purpose." Glimmers of this will probably start coming through ahead of the spiritual Dark Night of the Soul, and by the time you're fully integrated you'll be pretty sure why you came. This is because:

1) You've gathered insight and understanding about yourself at soul level during your journey, and

2) the universe wants you to uncover your purpose (so you can fulfil it), and will have sent you signs and clues along the way.

Finding our purpose is a process and can take time to work out. It took me well over a year to fully understand why I'm here. If it's the same for you, try not to overthink it. Worrying about our purpose is counter-productive and distracts us from focusing on our spiritual development. Rest assured, all will be revealed in time.

Your Purpose Will Be Something You Enjoy

If you're a higher evolved soul awakening at this time, without a doubt your purpose will center around something you enjoy. In these types of lives, the universe always picks the right person for the job, and will leverage your talents and experience (both from this life and others). In other words, it will fit a round peg into a round hole. That's one of the ways we know when we've found our purpose—it just feels "right."

If you find yourself pursuing a path which you think might be your purpose, but you start to feel unhappy, it's a signal that you're on the wrong track. Reappraise your absolute truths and your needs, does this path meet them? Almost certainly not, if it's making you miserable. It's fine to have a few false starts, the important thing is, you'll get there in the end.

Ultimately, your mission should inspire you, invigorate you, give you a sense of peace and purpose, be manageable to deliver, and leave you time to enjoy your life. It doesn't have to be huge, as long as it makes a difference. How big you go is up to you.

Finding Your Purpose During a Dark Night of the Soul

During a Dark Night of the Soul—either kind—it's natural to ask, "Why am I here?" and, "What's it all about?". Typically something feels lacking. We're looking for the thing that will give our life meaning, that thing that's bigger than ourselves. The kind of introspection engendered by a Dark Night means it's an opportune time to try to understand what this thing is.

My experience coaching others through their Dark Nights tells me that, at this stage of awakening, we often have an inkling of the path we need to follow but rarely have the whole picture. This eventually emerges via a process of self-examination, conversation with our guides, research, and experimentation. I would suggest that the first of these factors—self-examination—is a perfect exercise during the Dark Night of the Soul. You will (hopefully) already be doing a lot of this anyway, as part of your ongoing inner work.

Finding Your Purpose Through Self-Examination

If you identify with any of the following statements, it's a good indication that you're not yet fulfilling your purpose:

- you dislike your job, and it makes you unhappy;
- even if you enjoy your work, it doesn't fulfil you;
- you have a talent that's not being used day-to-day;
- your current job doesn't reflect the interests you had as a child;
- people comment you should be doing something else;
- there's a career you dream of having;
- you feel restless and under-utilized.

If this sounds like you, there's an exercise you can do to help you get closer to finding your purpose:

Exercise: Get Closer to Finding Your Purpose

Make a list of the causes that are important to you and the changes you would like to see in the world. Then make a list of your abilities, talents, and experiences—is there a way you could use these to improve the things you care about? If you are a higher evolved soul come to help, then your purpose will always be a confluence of these things. Try to think large-scale. It's more likely you have incarnated to help large situations or groups of people than to do something "one-on-one". But remember, you should enjoy your purpose, so always keep this in mind.

***

Why Can't My Guides Just Tell Me My Purpose?

There's two answers to this question. Even outside of the Dark Night of the Soul, with full communication, your guides are limited in the information they can provide. This is because:

1) the rules of the Game of Life restrict the amount of explicit direction our teams can give, to make the game more difficult and enjoyable;

2) we are the CEOs of our own lives and it's up to us to decide how we want to spend them—we might not *want* to pursue the purpose we originally intended for ourselves, once we've incarnated.

However, what your team *can* do, is confirm or encourage your own thoughts and decisions. If you can get yourself a fair way along the path towards understanding your purpose, then they'll be able to speak more openly to you about it. This is especially true if you've started taking action.

Chapter 10—Creative Protocols

The act of creation is one of the most effective ways to stimulate integration with your higher self. It's almost as powerful as a formal meditation practice. The reason? Creation strengthens and engages the right side of your brain, which is the material tool of your superconscious, and a direct route to your higher self.

Personally, I'm mad about art. I painted from an early age but stopped in my mid-twenties. Even though I was no longer painting, for many years afterwards I told people, "I'm an artist." Deep down I knew this to be the truth, but I didn't understand the conviction for what it was—I was sensing my true soul nature. In my mid-forties, I started to question—can I tell people I'm an artist if I don't make art? So, I took up the brush again and within seconds of making a mark on the canvas, I knew I was "supposed" to paint. Considering how potent a tool art is in the process of integration, it's no coincidence I went for so long creating nothing, or that I started painting again a year or two before my conscious spiritual awakening kicked in. My team were controlling the timing of my journey.

Almost all higher evolved souls intending to awaken in this life will have some sort of creative hobby or talent. This is exactly so your team can get you to a certain point of integration leading up to your conscious awakening (as they did with me). Without knowing it, you've been integrating with your higher self whenever you've spent time creating—even when you were scribbling in your coloring book as a child. This kind of "integration by stealth" is also the reason so many artists have such a strong spiritual leaning. Famous examples of this are Paul Klee, Wassily Kandinsky, and Vincent Van Gogh.

I give the example of art here, but there are many different ways to create—perhaps infinite ways. Finding the one which suits you will accelerate the integration process and be a great tool in speeding up your progress through the Dark Night of the Soul. You don't need to be a creative prodigy, you just need to enjoy it.

***

Protocol 35: Get Creating

All souls are creative beings, and we are all souls. Therefore, I guarantee that you have at least one creative skill you can draw on in your current incarnation, maybe more. Sometimes we decide to suppress this part of ourselves when we incarnate into a human life so we can learn, but since you are reading this book, that's unlikely to be your situation. So, what's your creative skill?

Whatever it is, please find time to practice it. You will enjoy it and aid integration at the same time. Creation is a broad area and includes anything that requires you to use the right side of your brain in a focused activity. Here's a list of activities that you could explore:

- drawing;
- painting;
- printing;
- origami;
- sculpture;
- pottery;
- making stained glass;
- knitting;
- crocheting;

- felting;
- weaving;
- dressmaking;
- embroidery;
- quilting;
- woodworking;
- model-making;
- candle-making;
- soap-making;
- jewelry-making;
- interior design;
- textile design;
- dancing;
- playing a musical instrument;
- DJing.

The list is potentially endless.

With so many creative pursuits to select from, there should be something which resonates with you. I would encourage you to try some out, especially if you're experiencing a Dark Night, they will really help. There's a reason people use art as therapy!

***

Protocol 36: Immerse Yourself in Music

The creation and enjoyment of music is also a right-brained activity, but I've given it its own section as it's a broad topic and there are deeper benefits associated with this creative discipline. Listening to music, playing an instrument, and DJing, can all enhance wellbeing and support integration with your higher self.

More than any other field of the arts, music resonates with us—literally. All sound is vibration and we, ourselves, vibrate according to our energetic frequency. That means that sounds which correspond to our own vibrations are appealing and healing. Music that's slower than our own vibration will calm us down; music which is faster will rev us up.

Music During a Dark Night of the Soul

During a Dark Night of the Soul is the perfect time to listen to old, favourite tunes, especially those that soothe you. In fact, you may find you can only listen to slow, gentle music, because during this time your own vibrational energy is "depressed"—you're vibrating more slowly. Fast, loud, or brash music may feel overwhelming—you can't accommodate the level of vibration it engenders. This is also true for a different reason in the period of intense connection, just before the spiritual Dark Night of the Soul. Your chakras are wide open and you're vibrating at a high rate. Loud, fast music will spiral you rapidly upwards, uncontrollably. This makes this sort of music intolerable at that time.

It's worth experimenting with music during the Dark Night (and at other times) to learn to use it to calibrate your mood and energy levels. For example, if you feel lethargic, choosing songs that are a level or two up from your vibrational rate can act as a pick-me-up. If you're experiencing heightened emotions, playing songs a step or two down will calm you.

We Are Drawn to Music Similar to Our Own Energetic Fingerprint

Another factor that comes into play, is that music from different artists carries a unique energetic fingerprint. Almost all (if not all) successful artists are higher evolved, old souls, from high up in the soul tree. That means some of them will figure somewhere in your own family tree—your soul is one of their soul's descendants.

We're most drawn to those artists we're related to at a soul level because we share energetic similarities. That's one reason we can become so attached to particular performers and so averse to others. In the latter instance, these are people far removed from us on the soul tree and with whom we therefore have a "discordant" energy pattern.

The contemporary musicians you admire today will have lived former lives as artists, or at least their souls have. The music created by the human avatars of their souls in each of these lives shares similar patterns. This can be heard in the example of Amy Winehouse, Nina Simone, and Billie Holiday; they were all avatars of the same soul. (Nina Simone was still alive when Amy Winehouse died, but remember, our souls incarnate in multiple human bodies at the same time. Just because human lives overlap doesn't mean they don't share the same soul. I appreciate this concept is difficult to grasp but we already have a version of it on Earth—the idea of the "Twin Flame.")

Messages Are Conveyed to Us in the Lyrics of Songs

Another reason to immerse yourself in music during the Dark Night (and indeed at any time), is that your team will sometimes send you messages via lyrics. They put the right songs in your way at the right time, to give you direction, reassurance, or support, either via a playlist, the radio, or someone playing a song for you they think you should hear. Sometimes hearing words of a song at a pivotal moment can change the course of our direction. Other times they can deliver profound comfort.

Our Taste in Music Changes as We Develop

Music is intended by the universe as an accompaniment to our lives, to inspire, soothe, heal, and energize. Depending where we are in our spiritual journey, different artists and genres will appeal to us at different times, because our vibrational needs change. Your team influences this, trying to make sure we get what we need from music, when we need it.

Our Teams Have a Fun Game They Like to Play With Music

Our teams in the higher dimensions are maneuvering and manifesting on our behalf constantly. They try to line things up so they fall into place at the right time. I'm sure you've had an experience when the thing you needed, however big or small, manifested at the moment you required it. This is a prized skill in Soul World and gives rise to a great deal of friendly competition. Our teams like to practice and hone their ability in this area by playing a fun game.

In this game, they line up your actions, thoughts, or words, with the song that is playing, so they correspond. I'll give you a quick example. Recently, I was painting in the studio and it was getting warm. However, I was so immersed in what I was doing, I hadn't drunk anything and I was aware I was thirsty. Suddenly, the thought popped into my mind—"Water!" (Planted by my higher self, of course). At the same time, the first line of the Talking Heads version of "Take Me to the River" boomed through the speaker. My thought, "Water!" coincided with David Byrne singing the exact same word. This is just one example but I've had many similar experiences.

Once you become attuned to this little game, you'll spot it being played frequently (our teams do it with TV shows too). It gives me immense pleasure to know they're enjoying themselves—even though it's sometimes at my expense. If you want to give your team the chance to show you what they can do, create a playlist with plenty of songs on it to give them a bit of scope, and then set it going on the "random" setting. I guarantee you'll experience some interesting "coincidences."

Exercise: Create a Playlist

If you don't already have a suitable one, create a playlist on Spotify, Apple Music, or another app. Choose at least fifty songs you love, by a variety of artists, which have lyrics. Include some favorites from when you were younger. The next time you're doing something—cooking, cleaning, creating—put the playlist on in the background and wait for the game to begin.

***

Chapter 11—Giving Back Protocols

This last group of protocols encourages you to turn outwards and focus on the people around you. Again, it may be something you decide to do after you've exited the Dark Night of the Soul, depending on your energy level and capacity for social interaction. But if you can muster the strength to do something in this space during a Dark Night, it's beneficial.

All souls are co-operative beings. As I've mentioned a few times in this book, helping one another is the entire foundation soul society is based on, in the higher dimensions. The Earth is catching up to this idea. When we do things "true" to us at soul level, we feel good. That's why giving to charity (for example) gives us a boost. Plus, you will spend so much time in your head during the Dark Night, whichever type it is, you'll find it a relief to focus on other people for a change.

Protocol 37: Do Things for Others

It's important that we do things for others to support our spiritual development, however, helping other people is a skill. We have to make sure we're not trying to give more than we can realistically offer, and we need to know we're the right person for the job. There's an unwritten rule in the universe that doing things for other people should be easy. Our teams arrange matters so there's always someone available who can help solve a problem. Sometimes we're the helpee and sometimes we're the helper. They organize everything so that one of us holds the right "answer key" for the exact "problem lock." If you find it difficult to aid someone with a particular issue, you're not the person with the key. In that case, it's fine to say you're unable to help, or to offer an alternative solution that's easier for you to commit to. Often we know someone who's better placed to help and can put them in touch.

The challenge we have in earthly society, is that things are unbalanced. Not everyone gives help and not everyone asks for it. As higher evolved souls, and therefore guides and teachers, we're inclined to help others, even if they haven't solicited our support. This means we can easily give too much and become drained, which is no good for our individual or collective health. So, the guidelines for doing things for others are:

- either wait for them to ask for help, or
- offer your help just once and leave it up to them to accept it, and
- give things that are easy for you to offer but are of benefit to the other person. This will prevent you from becoming stretched too thin while still being able to help.

If there are people in your life who take more than they give and who drain your resources, it's OK to say no. In fact, you should. It's important to draw boundaries and protect your energy levels. This is a hard lesson for higher evolved souls whose instinct is to give, give, give—especially if they descend from Om, Sophia, Michael, Freya, or Isis on the soul tree. The question to ask yourself is, "how much am I helping the collective soul community"? If you're exhausting yourself, you're not helping the collective. If you're preventing someone from learning because you're taking up their slack, you're not helping the collective. This is a nuanced area, but with practice you'll be able to judge when to give help and when not.

Top Up Your Karma Points

Assuming you get the calibration right, another reason to do things for others is that it tops up your "karma points." Yep, karma is a thing. It means "balance." In the great scorebook of life, everything you do is assessed as neutral, positive, or negative. This assessment is based on whether your actions caused harm or benefit to others, or had no impact either way (neutral). Your net "score" corresponds to your karma points. The idea is to accrue a positive balance so your team can spend your reserves when they need to. They can use your points to bring you benefits (we construe this as "luck"), or send you direct messages when otherwise the rules of the Game of Life would prevent it.

When we perform good deeds (or bad), the rules of karma dictate we'll always receive the corresponding number of points back, whether positive or negative. Here's a quick example of how it works: if you lend someone in need money when you have little yourself and they don't pay you back, that money will still return to you later down the line, even though it comes from a different source. Sometimes it won't be repaid in money, but in another way, corresponding in value. It's the same for everything; every deed will eventually be "balanced out." And if it doesn't get repaid in this lifetime, it will carry over into your subsequent lifetimes. There's only one way to erase karma points which are owed, and that's through forgiveness. If we emotionally write off that which is due to us, then the debt is cleared.

If you stay aware, it's possible to observe karma in action every day, especially between you and your friends, family, colleagues, and neighbors, who are often members of your soul group. Your team will try to keep you all in neutral balance as you continue through this lifetime, so they can be sure there'll be no need for you to reincarnate specifically to pay off a "karmic debt." For this reason you'll find there's always an opportunity to repay someone for a kindness they have done to you.

Not keeping up this discipline of repaying our debts is how people can get locked into a spiral of reincarnating lives driven by karma. This is one reason you should embrace opportunities to help others—it may be your team presenting you with a way to balance your debt or increase your points reserve. I have noticed that, when someone goes out of their way for me, within a week or two, an occasion arises in which I can do something similar in return—not always for them directly, but a comparable act that will benefit someone, somewhere.

I make sure I keep my karma points topped up, by doing proactive "good deeds" here and there when I see an opportunity. This could be as simple as feeding the feral cats in my neighborhood or depositing a load of clothes at the charity shop, as well as specific acts of kindness to individuals. Of course, it's possible that someone has incarnated in this life to help you in your mission and to pay off a debt they incurred in a previous incarnation. Sometimes this lifetime and the one in which they owed you can be centuries apart. In fact, I'm aware of a couple of people in my life where this is the case. They have helped me in my journey this time around and so discharged their debt.

The farther you proceed through your awakening, the more you will sense these relationships and imbalances and know when to give and when to take (graciously and gratefully).

Exercise: Top Up Your Karma Points

Write a list of small things you can do easily which will help others. "Others" includes individuals, charities, social groups, animals, and the planet. Depending on your energy levels, try to perform small kindnesses a few times a week.

***

Protocol 38: Find Ways to be Useful

As a higher evolved soul, you're here to be "useful", that's your destiny. However, there are other benefits to making ourselves useful. For example, it's a route to improved self-esteem and a sense of "actualization," so it can be a real tonic when going through a Dark Night of the Soul.

This protocol is similar to the previous one but different in scale. I'm speaking less of one-to-one support and more of finding something you can do that will have a significantly wider impact. Whether or not you're aware of it, you're talented, connected, and experienced. You have something to offer that's unique to you. Without a doubt, you can make a difference in this world. Even small things, taken together, add up to something big.

The best way to be useful is to play to your strengths. What is the thing you could do, at scale, that would benefit more than one person? When you think about how you can contribute, opportunities will present themselves. It doesn't mean you have to take every chance that comes your way but, if you follow up on just one or two, soon you'll see: you have made a difference.

Again, if you're going through a spiritual Dark Night of the Soul, you may choose to wait until you're out of the other side before looking for a project. However, there's no harm (and a lot of good) in thinking about areas in which you could be useful in the future. You can also link this to the work you're doing to uncover your life's purpose. Finding a mini-project could be a springboard into something bigger that leads you to your true path.

If you're going through a growth-oriented Dark Night, using your abilities to make the world a better place can be a powerful tool to pull you out of your slump. Looking beyond your own challenges will make your problems seem smaller, build your self-esteem, collect a few karma points, and give you a warm, fuzzy glow. As always, with both types of Dark Night, make sure you aren't spreading yourself too thin.

Exercise: Find Ways to Be Useful

Find some quiet time to think through these two questions. 1) What skills or knowledge do you have which could be used to benefit a wider group of people? 2) What opportunities can you see around you where you could put these to good use? Once you have pinpointed these two things, write down at least one thing you will do to take action.

***

Protocol 39: Communicate Your Experience

Talking About Your Experience of the Spiritual Dark Night of the Soul

If you're going through a spiritual Dark Night of the Soul, you have volunteered to be one of the Earth's earliest conscious awakeners. Stop and think about this. There are almost eight billion people on planet Earth and only five percent will go through a conscious spiritual awakening before the end of 2027. So, you're a trailblazer, a torch-bearer, an illuminator of the path. That means you *have* to talk about your experience. Not only will you encourage others to push on with their journey, but you'll inspire the next wave of awakeners to take the first step on the path to enlightenment. The more people who awaken, the more peaceful, tolerant, compassionate, and loving our Earth society will be. Yes, it's an enormous responsibility, but you're more than up to the task. That's why you offered to do this.

It's difficult being the first to do something and you may be shy of talking about your experience. The process of conscious awakening is so new to Earth, it's natural to worry—"Will people understand? Will they ridicule me?" Even worse, "Will people think I'm crazy?" I had the same fears. However, once I realized I was travelling a pioneering path along which others would soon follow, I understood I had a duty to talk about it. As I said, we're here to guide. In this instance, *we* are the teachers who appear when the students are ready.

A defining feature of this early cohort of awakeners is we tend to be naturally humble and averse to self-promotion. This is deliberate. Imagine if all the power that full conscious awakening bestows was handed to megalomaniacs. The Earth would soon be in a far worse state than it currently is. Getting over this barrier is essential to helping others with their own journeys to enlightenment. It was one I had to hurdle myself. When I feel myself avoiding publicity (making videos, for example), I remind myself that Jesus only ever wanted to be a carpenter. However, he understood and accepted that he came to do something far bigger, and so taught himself to become a public speaker. He would spend hours honing and rehearsing his parables, overcoming his natural inclination towards a quiet, reserved life. You will find, once you get into your stride, you enjoy sharing your message. The higher evolved are natural teachers and relish helping others progress. Keep this in mind, always.

While I was going through the initial stages of my awakening, for a long time I told only a few people what was happening to me, and even then, only snippets. Most reactions ranged from embarrassment, to disbelief, to concern. However, a minority of people—an important minority—understood and told me about their own experiences, or those of someone they knew. Often they related that they were in the early stages of awakening themselves. In fact, it surprised me how many people reported symptoms of awakening. It's really happening, we are actually waking up…and more quickly than I imagined.

So, it became apparent to me that there's an urgent need out there for information, encouragement, and support. If the global spiritual awakening is going to succeed, then we need to talk about our own spiritual journeys, whatever stage we're at.

Talking About Your Experience of a Growth-Oriented Dark Night of the Soul

If you're going through a growth-oriented Dark Night of the Soul, it's still vitally important to talk about your experience, especially when you have resolved your situation. You have powerful advice to offer which can inspire others going through the same thing. And remember, no-one can start the conscious awakening journey without untangling their "human" issues through inner work, so every individual you encourage to move forwards with their self-development is a potential future awakener.

Ways to Talk About Your Experience

There has never been a better time to talk about personal experience. There's an enormous trend toward self-improvement and interest in "ordinary" people's lives. The exponential rise in the popularity of "quit lit" and personal memoirs is testament to that.

It has also never been easier to get your message out there. You have the entire digital landscape of social media, blogs, e-courses, and podcasts to facilitate your communication, as well as "real-world" opportunities such as motivational speaking. Or you could write a book, as I've done. If you're struggling to get over the mental barrier to broadcasting your experiences, you can at least commit to giving an honest answer to anyone who asks you about your journey. The receptiveness and responses you receive will surprise you.

***

Protocol 40: Celebrate!

OK, this isn't quite about "giving back," but it's important and I wanted to include it, so…. Believe it or not, if you're going through a Dark Night of the Soul, you have much to celebrate. Why? If you're going through a spiritual Dark Night, the cause for celebration should be easy to see, even if you can't "feel" it yet. You are part of something huge and transformative that will improve the life of every single human being on Earth, now, and long after you've departed this realm. You are one of a few individuals pioneering this life-changing experience today. The future waiting for you on the other side of the Dark Night is better than you ever imagined.

And of course, once you've navigated the Dark Night, there's even more cause for celebration, because you'll be part of a tiny minority who have achieved this feat. Congratulations! Be proud of yourself.

If you're going through a growth-oriented Dark Night of the Soul, you still have things to celebrate. You are here; you didn't give up; you have the strength to do something about it (that's why you're reading this book). The universe has given you the opportunity to re-examine yourself and your life and make changes that will lead to a happier, more fulfilling future... *you are on the cusp of transformation.*

I know it's almost impossible to think of celebrating while in the throes of a Dark Night of the Soul, and that's fine. But there's no harm in thinking about how you will reward yourself once you've navigated your way through. Make it something big—you worked hard for this!

Chapter 12—How to Incorporate the Protocols into Your Life

In the second half of this book I provided forty protocols to help you get through the Dark Night of the Soul, or progress your spiritual journey, whichever stage you're at. I appreciate it may feel overwhelming. Don't worry, you don't need to do everything all at once, and you'll find some protocols work better for you than others—we're all individuals.

Below I provide a simple step by step roadmap for incorporating these protocols into your life. Take it slowly and only move onto the next stage when you feel ready. Habits are easier to form one by one, don't try to do everything all at once. If you slip back for a week or two, don't worry or get frustrated. Just re-gather your energy and start again when you feel ready.

If I can get through the Dark Night of the Soul by adopting these protocols, you can too. You will discover you enjoy living in a spiritual way and it will feel natural to you very quickly.

Incorporating the Protocols into the Growth-Oriented Dark Night—Introduction

During the growth-oriented Dark Night, the focus should be on changing self-limiting behaviors and circumstances. It's also important to be kind to ourselves and reprogram negative thought patterns. The roadmap I outline below is designed to do these three things but please include any other protocols you feel drawn to.

Similarly, if there's a protocol you don't feel ready for, leave that one and move onto the next, or replace it with something you feel better able to do. Please note: I am not a doctor. If your situation is serious, please seek medical advice.

Growth-Oriented Dark Night—Incorporating Protocols: Stage 1

These protocols focus on building a healthy physical platform for future work.

Protocol 3: Be Kind to Yourself

Set aside time each day to do something nice for yourself. Have an indulgent bath, treat yourself to a delicious (healthy) meal, read a few pages of a favorite book.

Protocol 7: Get Rid of Addictive Substances

Start the process to exclude these from your life, or at least cut down significantly. This will take time so may continue into stages two and three.

Protocol 8: Eat a Healthy Diet

Reduce processed and sugary foods in your diet. Try to cut down on caffeine and red meat if you're a meat-eater. Make sure you are getting some fruit and vegetables every day. Buy organic if you can.

Protocol 9: Take Supplements

If you can afford it, seek the advice of a qualified nutritional therapist. Otherwise, take a high quality multi-vitamin each day. Magnesium will also help with your energy levels. Consider supplements such as St John's Wort for depression but only if you're not already taking anti-depressants.

Protocol 10: Spend Time in Nature

Try to get outdoors every day, into a green space if possible. Turn your face up to the sun for at least a few moments.

Protocol 20: Practice grounding

Reduce anxiety by performing a grounding exercise every morning, and whenever you need it during the day.

Growth-Oriented Dark Night—Incorporating Protocols: Stage 2

These Protocols focus on increasing happiness and helping you start to identify new opportunities, building on the stable platform you created in Stage 1.

Protocol 35: Get Creating

Find a new creative hobby, or spend time doing something you already enjoy.

Protocol 36: Immerse Yourself in Music

Create playlists to suit your moods. Listen to them regularly. Turn the music up loud.

Protocol 26: Keep a Diary

Start to document your experience and moods. Review your previous diary entries regularly to spot patterns.

Protocol 16: Meditate Daily

If you don't meditate, now's the time to start. Meditating will stabilise your mood and provide flashes of insight to help you in your journey.

Protocol 21: Practice Gratitude

A regular gratitude practice will elevate your mood.

Protocol 23: Ask the Universe For Help

Get in the habit of asking for your team's help. Be explicit about what you need.

Growth-Oriented Dark Night—Incorporating Protocols: Stage 3

These Protocols start the process of change in yourself and your life.

Protocol 32: Assess Your Life

Conduct a life audit. You don't need to make a plan at this point (Protocol 33) but if you feel up to it, go for it. The aim is to understand what isn't working for you.

Protocol 28: Do Your Inner Work

You've now created a more stable, healthy, happy platform for your system, so it's a good time to start of progress your inner work.

Protocols 29 and 30: Consider Therapy / Find a Coach or Teacher

If you feel you need extra support during your inner work journey, find that person.

Protocol 27: Research

Whatever you need to find out more about, research it at this point. Remember, knowledge is power.

Protocol 33: Make a Plan

When you feel ready, make a plan. It only needs to be for a few steps ahead. The important thing is you know where you want to get to.

Growth-Oriented Dark Night—What to Do Once You've Completed These Stages

Some habits will bed in more easily than others. Without being too hard on yourself, assess which areas you want to do more work on, and which you think are already an established part of your routine.

If and when you want to develop further, you could follow the stages for the Spiritual Dark Night of the Soul below. These already assume a fairly stable emotional platform and are centered on advanced spiritual growth, although there will be some overlap.

Incorporating the Protocols into the Spiritual Dark Night—Introduction

If you're in a Spiritual Dark Night of the Soul, necessarily you will already have completed a lot of your inner work and will be using some of the protocols in this book. This stage of the awakening journey is about "doubling down" and committing to a spiritual routine which will aid faster integration with your higher self. During this period you will benefit from trying to adhere to your practice 100 percent, but as always, be kind to yourself. It's ok to have an off day.

Having said that, the stages I outline below assume you have significant capabilities. If you're going through a spiritual Dark Night of the Soul, we know you're a higher evolved being. That means you should have the capacity to take on more. Detachment is your friend during this period. Learn to push the negative feelings to one side, elevate your mind, and plough on through. You can do it.

Spiritual Dark Night—Incorporating Protocols: Stage 1

These protocols focus on establishing a basic platform to support ongoing integration.

Protocol 16: Meditate Daily

As often as possible, for as long as possible, even if you can't feel the connection. This is your primary tool of integration, so prioritise it.

Protocol 8: Eat a Spiritual Diet

During a spiritual Dark Night of the Soul, it's important to eliminate anything which will prevent you integrating and ascending. Cutting the "wrong" things out of your diet and including the "right" things is a part of this.

Protocol 7: Get Rid of Addictive Substances

As with the protocol above, eliminate anything you're putting into your system which is preventing you elevating your mind.

Protocol 31: Get Rid of Bad Habits

If you have any self-limiting behaviors left, now's the time to work on them.

Protocol 10: Spend Time in Nature

Try to combine this with walking meditation.

Protocol 4: Rest, a Lot

Rest is crucial during the spiritual Dark Night of the Soul. Get plenty of sleep and don't feel bad about reducing your activity.

Protocol 1: Accept the Situation You're In

Accepting that this is a temporary stage of the awakening journey that you have no choice but to push through, will give you the determination to keep going.

Protocol 2: Remember What's Waiting for You on the Other Side

Re-read the list in Chapter 4 regularly as an encouragement to continue.

Protocol 24: Talk to Your Team Even if You Feel They're Not Listening

Remember, you're in this together.

Spiritual Dark Night—Incorporating Protocols: Stage 2

These additional Protocols will accelerate your integration and shorten the length of time the Dark Night endures.

Protocol 6: Decide to Succeed

Program your system to believe you will get through the Dark Night of the Soul.

Protocol 21: Practice Gratitude

Lift your spirits by using gratitudes, even if you don't feel grateful at this moment in time. Use the specific suite of gratitudes for the spiritual Dark Night which I provide in Protocol 21.

Protocol 19: Use Energy Clearing Exercises

Daily energy clearing will help accelerate integration and lift your mood during the spiritual Dark Night of the Soul, even if only slightly.

Protocol 22: Use Affirmations and Visualizations

Focus these on getting through the Dark Night of the Soul.

Protocol 23: Ask the Universe For Help

Again, ask for help in getting through the Dark Night.

Protocol 35: Get Creating

Spend as much time as your schedule and energy levels will allow in creative pursuits. This will dramatically speed up integration with your higher self.

Spiritual Dark Night—Incorporating Protocols: Stage 3

These protocols focus on helping you to identify your mission and make a plan for when you are through the Dark Night.

Protocol 32: Assess Your Life

What isn't working for you? What change do you need to see? What are your absolute truths?

Protocol 34: Find Your Purpose

Why are you here? What did you intend to do in this lifetime?

Protocol 33: Make a Plan

How will you make the changes you need to start the journey towards your purpose? Ask your team for help.

Protocol 38: Find Ways to be Useful

How can you put your skills and experience to good use? Are there small things you can do which will make a big difference to others?

Protocol 26: Keep a Diary or Blog

As a way-shower, your experiences during the spiritual Dark Night of the Soul have the potential to shine a light for others. You may not remember everything in hindsight, so start keeping a journal now.

Protocol 39: Communicate Your Experience

In whichever way suits you best, share your Dark Night experience. Millions of people could potentially benefit.

Spiritual Dark Night—What to Do Once You're Out the Other Side

If you stick to the protocols in Stages 1 and 2 outlined above, you should be out of the spiritual Dark Night of the Soul in a matter of months. The first thing to do is celebrate! How will you reward yourself for your perseverance? Pick something just for you.

Once you're on the other side of the Dark Night, it's imperative to keep going with a daily spiritual routine, otherwise you may slip backwards. However, feel free to return to the 80/20 rule and cut yourself some slack. You still have more integration to do but this part is a lot easier and far more enjoyable. I would focus during this time in developing communication with your guides and higher self. Learn or perfect a divination technique, experiment with lucid dreaming, try self-hypnosis. And of course, continue to meditate daily. The more you can establish clear two-way communication, the easier your path will be.

Incorporating the Protocols—Conclusion

Spiritual awakening is hard, but the benefits are life-transforming. Experimenting with these protocols and working out how best to fit them into your life will aid you on the spiritual journey. As with forming any new habits, it may take you a couple of go's to get it right. That's ok. Keep persevering and you will get there. Soon a spiritually-driven way of life will be second nature for you. I wish you every success.

Afterword

Writing this book has been a labor of love. I'm passionate about helping people through their spiritual awakenings—nothing gives me greater pleasure than to see others enjoy the spiritual benefits I feel so lucky to have.

If you're going through a Dark Night of the Soul, I know you will find your way through and to a happier, more fulfilling life. If I can do it, you can do it. Please have faith. Be kind to yourself. The journey can be hard, with many twists and turns, but I know you're up to the challenge. If you're taking two steps forward and one step back, so be it. As long as you're making some progress, you are on the right track.

Spiritual awakening is the most precious gift we can give ourselves as souls incarnated in human form—cherish and embrace it. Most of all, understand that you are an inspiration to others, with the power to change the future of the whole human race for the better.

I would like to end this book with a few words from Sophia, my higher self. She is my constant companion, my mentor, and my great friend, and her love for all souls is boundless. This is her message for you.

A Message from Sophia

Dearest souls, I am so proud of you. You have volunteered to do something extraordinarily difficult that is bigger than yourself. That takes courage and that takes heart. Thank you.

Whether you realize it or not at this moment, you are special. The future of the Earth is rich and beautiful, but we can't get there without you. If you are harboring self-doubt, don't. You are powerful, far more than you know. There is nothing you can't do and no trial you cannot overcome if you just believe in yourself, the way I believe in you.

Your guides are with you constantly and are there to help you. Draw on that help.

The protocols in this book will allow you to build deep and fruitful connections with them for your own and the greater good. If you commit to the spiritual path, you will soon discover that you are never alone and always supported. Then everything will feel easy. It's all within you. Dig deep and you will find it.

I and the other members of the Council of Light are immensely grateful for your commitment and your sacrifice. Please know that we will do everything in our power to assure your success, whatever path you choose to take.

With love,
Sophia.

A Request From The Author

I hope this book has been useful to you. It would really help if you left **a review on Amazon** so it has the best chance possible of reaching the people who need it.

Please also recommend or lend this book to others going through a Dark Night of the Soul. The future of the Earth depends on our successful collective awakening!

With love,
Sophia Persephone

Glossary

80/20 Rule: A balanced way of living which advocates adherence to "good" practices 80 percent of the time, while allowing the practitioner to relax the rules for the other 20 percent of the time.

Akashic Records: The universal database which contains every piece of information about our universe and the souls inhabiting it, past and present. It also contains projections for the future.

Autophagy: A self-healing process by which a cell breaks down and destroys old, damaged, or abnormal proteins and other substances in its cytoplasm. Autophagy is triggered by fasting i.e. going without food for extended periods of time.

Bodhisattva Soul: A soul who has completed at least 98 percent of their total soul learning (not just in this lifetime). I have borrowed this word from the Buddhists. A Bodhisattva soul no longer needs to incarnate on Earth to learn, instead they come to help propel the Game of Life forward to the next major story waypoint, either by taking on a substantial mission, or supporting others in theirs.

Conscious Mind: The mental domain of a soul incarnated in a human avatar.

Dimensions: Environments which souls inhabit and which range in type from the completely non-physical to the densely material. There are thirteen dimensions in our wider universe.

Ego: A part of the human avatar which collects beliefs about ourselves, generated from the moment we are born. These beliefs form much of the basis of our personality and attachments, prior to conscious spiritual awakening. The Ego's purpose is to give the human avatar a sense of homogenous identity prior to the discovery via awakening that the avatar is constructed of several parts, some of which exist multi-dimensionally.

Enlightenment: The state of being which results from spiritual awakening and denotes understanding and acceptance of ourselves as souls, existing in a multi-dimensional universe.

Epiphany: The moment of conscious spiritual awakening, when an awakener realises beyond all doubt that there is more to our universe than the Earth's 3D material reality, and more to us as beings than our physical bodies. An epiphany can be a sudden event, or a dawning of realisation over time.

Gamify: To make something more enjoyable by adding elements of a game to it, such as points collection, or having opposing teams competing against one another.

Generation Z: The youngest generation with adult members spanning birthdates between 1997 and 2013. This generation of souls is primed for awakening and they have incarnated with more natural awareness of their true spiritual nature than older generations.

Freya: A senior member of the Council of Light, and one of the original ten members from whom all souls are descended. She is most recognisable on Earth by one of her incarnations as the Norse goddess of Love, variously known as: Freya, Freyja, or Frigg.

Growth-Oriented Dark Night of the Soul: A period of spiritual depression occasioned by our own actions or inactions, or traumatic or damaging events.

Guide: A soul or spirit situated in a higher dimension who is assigned to help you in your Earthly journey. Your higher self is one of your guides and you are permanently connected. You also have a primary guide who may change over time, depending on your needs and mission. At least one guide always accompanies you.

Higher Dimensions: The environments which are higher up than the Earthly plane. Earth exists on the third dimension from the bottom, so there are ten "higher" dimensions. All of these dimensions have already attained enlightenment.

Higher Evolved: Souls who have completed a significant portion of their entire soul learning, not just the lessons from this one life. I use this term to denote beings whose lessons are at least 70 percent complete.

Higher Self: The soul your soul is "birthed" from. Exactly as with a human parent, we inherit characteristics from our higher self. They remain in the higher dimensions but we have a permanent connection to them while we're incarnated on Earth.

Human Avatar: The collective minds of an incarnated soul, higher self, body, and Ego, housed in a physical shell which we currently understand on Earth as a "human being". A soul will have many human avatars in its lifetime, as it reincarnates.

Intermittent Fasting: An eating protocol which restricts the amount of hours in a day a person takes in food. Leaving a longer time without eating allows the body to repair itself via a process called "autophagy."

Karma: The process of scoring every deed of every soul as neutral, positive, or negative, and ensuring debts are repaid between souls. Karma literally means "balance." The idea is that ultimately, all souls will be in karmic balance, owing nothing.

Karma Points: The points which are awarded or subtracted when our deeds are scored, according to the rules of karma. The net number represents our pot of karma points, which, if it's in positive balance, our team can use to help us.

Keeper: A soul, usually higher evolved, whose mission it is in their lifetime to take care of another soul going through a conscious spiritual awakening. They may volunteer to do this because they have a karmic debt to repay, typically from a previous incarnation. The Keeper provides financial and circumstantial security, to allow the awakener time and space to go through the most turbulent stages of the journey. They are often a romantic partner. However, the relationship may end once the awakener is through the spiritual Dark Night of the Soul, as after this point they need to move on to the company of other souls who are also awakening, which a Keeper rarely does.

Lower Dimensions: Earth and the two dimensions below it, which are densely physical and not yet enlightened.

Multi-Dimensional Being: Souls are multi-dimensional beings, which means they exist in more than one dimension at once. This is the case because souls are able to replicate or split into exact copies of themselves, for example, so they can send part of themselves to Earth to incarnate in a human avatar.

Nirvana: A transcendent state in which there is neither suffering, desire, nor sense of self, and the subject is released from the effects of karma and the cycle of death and rebirth. The reality of this for Earth would mean universal peace and the ability to live an eternal life on this plane.

Om: A senior member of the Council of Light, and one of the original ten members from whom all souls are descended. His name means "love" and he is present today on Earth in the sacred sound "Om" used in meditation by some major religions and traditions, such as Hinduism and Buddhism. Along with Sophia, Om is the main overseer of the Earth Project.

OMAD: A form of intermittent fasting during which the practitioner eats only One Meal A Day, thereby fasting for almost twenty-four hours.

Oversoul: Interchangeable with the term "higher self."

Sophia: A senior member of the Council of Light, and one of the original ten members from whom all souls are descended. She is most recognisable on Earth by one of her incarnations as the Greek Goddess of Love and Wisdom. In Gnosticism she is understood as one of the female aspects of God and in Christian tradition is represented by the Holy Spirit.

Soul: A non-physical being which travels through all of the dimensions, with the purpose of learning, often taking on a physical form so it can interact with the lower, material dimensions, such as the Earthly Plane.

Soul World: The collective higher dimensions above the dimension where Earth is situated.

Spirit: A non-material version of a human avatar which persists after death and resides in the higher dimensions. Previous avatars of our own soul often act as our guides.

Spiritual: Pertaining to souls and soul nature.

Spiritual Awakening: The process of reconnecting our soul to our higher self from our position on Earth, by integrating the conscious and superconscious minds.

Spiritual Dark Night of the Soul: A period of spiritual depression which is hard-wired into the spiritual awakening process and which we must get through to attain full integration with our higher selves.

Story Waypoint: A milestone in the Game of Life which must be reached for the game to be able to move forward.

Subconscious Mind: The mental domain of our body.

Superconscious Mind: The mental domain of our higher self.

Synchronicity: A repetition of events or symbols designed to impart a message to us, typically instigated by our teams in the higher dimensions.

Team: The collection of beings who remain in the higher dimensions and who are assigned to help us through our earthly journeys. Our team includes our higher self and guides.

The Council of Light: The organisation which oversees our universe, headed up by ten senior, original souls who have existed since the beginning of time. All souls in our multi-dimensional universe are descended from one of the ten original members of the Council.

The Earth Project: The Game of Life as it directly pertains to Earth. The mission to steer Earth to enlightenment and beyond. The Earth Project is headed up by Om and Sophia.

The Earthly Plane: The dimension in which the Earth is situated.

The Game of Life: The gamification of life on Earth. A way of making our learning as souls more challenging and enjoyable. The Game of Life has strict rules and features two "opposing" teams.

The Other Side: Interchangeable with the term "Soul World."

The Soul Tree: The family tree of souls. All souls descend from one of the ten original members of The Council of Light, and inherit characteristics and preferences specific to that Council member.

Time: The phenomenon we experience on Earth as a forward progression of sequential events which can be measured in constant discrete units, such as seconds, minutes, and hours. In fact, time moves backwards and forwards and can over-write and re-write history, without us being aware of it. Also, in reality, time does not move at a constant speed, but can be faster or slower, depending on what function is being performed. For example, the formation of the universe moved at a far greater speed than the time we experience today. In addition, time moves more quickly in the higher dimensions than it does on Earth. One year of our time is approximately one day of theirs.

Time-Restricted Eating: Interchangeable with the term "intermittent fasting."

Unconscious Mind: The mental domain of our Ego.

Zen: Zen, or Zen philosophy, is a way of life which strives for perfection of the person, through "right thought" and "right deeds." It teaches that enlightenment is achieved through the realization that we are already enlightened beings (in other words, rediscovering our true soul natures). Meditation is a foundational plank of this philosophy, in fact, Zen literally means "meditation".

Recommended Reading

During a Dark Night of the Soul, or at any stage of the awakening journey, read as much as you can. You will be drawn to certain topics—follow these threads. Below I provide a selection of books which I personally found particularly helpful through my awakening. They cover a relatively broad range of topics and many of them are written by scientists. If you decide to read them for yourselves, I hope you find them useful.

Recommended Reading: Health, Diet, and Self-Development

Gary Taubes. 2010. *Why We Get Fat: And What to Do About.* Anchor.
Dr. Robert H. Lustig. 2013. *Fat Chance: Beating the Odds Against Sugar, Processed Food, Obesity, and Disease.* Avery.
Jason Fung, M.D. 2016. *The Obesity Code - Unlocking the Secrets of Weight Loss.* Greystone Books.
Robynne Chutkan. 2016. *The Microbiome Solution: A Radical New Way to Heal Your Body from the Inside Out.* Avery.
Martin J. Blaser, M.D. 2015. *Missing Microbes: How the Overuse of Antibiotics Is Fueling Our Modern Plagues.* Picador.
Michael Greger, M.D. 2015. *How Not to Die: Discover the Foods Scientifically Proven to Prevent and Reverse Disease.* Flatiron Books.
Nathaniel Branden. 2012. *The Six Pillars of Self-Esteem.*
Peter Hollins. 2017. *The Science of Self-Discipline: The Willpower, Mental Toughness, and Self-Control to Resist Temptation and Achieve Your Goals (Live a Disciplined Life Book 1).*

Recommended Reading: Science and Medicine

Michael Pollan. 2018. *How to Change Your Mind: What the New Science of Psychedelics Teaches Us About Consciousness, Dying, Addiction, Depression, and Transcendence.* Penguin Press. (This book was made into a Netflix documentary in 2022.)
Dr Richard Louis Miller. 2017. *Psychedelic Medicine: The Healing Powers of LSD, MDMA, Psilocybin, and Ayahuasca.* Park Street Press.
Ben Goldacre. 2010. *Bad Science: Quacks, Hacks, and Big Pharma Flacks.* Farrar, Straus and Giroux.
Ben Goldacre. 2014. *Bad Pharma: How Drug Companies Mislead Doctors and Harm Patients.* Farrar, Straus and Giroux.
Marc Lewis PhD. 2016. *The Biology of Desire: Why Addiction Is Not a Disease.* PublicAffairs.
Bruce H. Lipton, PhD. 2010. *The Biology Of Belief : Unleashing The Power Of Consciousness, Matter & Miracles.* Hay House.
Iain McGilchrist.2019. *The Master and His Emissary: The Divided Brain and the Making of the Western World.* Yale University Press.
Peter Wohlleben. 2016. *The Hidden Life of Trees: What They Feel, How They Communicate—Discoveries from A Secret World (The Mysteries of Nature, 1).* Greystone Books.
Merlin Sheldron. 2021. *Entangled Life: How Fungi Make Our Worlds, Change Our Minds & Shape Our Futures.* Random House Trade Paperbacks.

Recommended Reading: Sociological, Anthropological, Ethical

Adam Rutherford. 2018. *A Brief History of Everyone Who Ever Lived: The Human Story Retold Through Our Genes.* The Experiment.
Michael Pollan. 2007. *The Omnivore's Dilemma: A Natural History of Four Meals.* Penguin Press.
Jonathan Safran Foer. 2010. *Eating Animals.* Back Bay Books.

Yuval Noah Harari. 2018. *Sapiens: A Brief History of Humankind*. Random House Harper.

Johann Hari. 2016. *Chasing the Scream: The First and Last Days of the War on Drugs*. Bloomsbury Publishing.

Johann Hari. 2018. *Lost Connections: Uncovering the Real Causes of Depression - and the Unexpected Solutions*. Bloomsbury Publishing.

Recommended Reading: Quantum Physics

Philip Ball. 2018. *Beyond Weird*. Vintage Digital.

Carlo Rovelli. 2016. *Reality Is Not What It Seems: The Journey to Quantum Gravity*. Penguin Press.

Chad Orzel. 2010. *How to Teach Quantum Physics to Your Dog*. Oneworld Publications.

Recommended Reading: Reincarnation

Morey Bernstein. 2010. *The Search for Bridey Murphy*. Transworld Digital.

Ian Stevenson, M.D. 2016. *Children Who Remember Previous Lives: A Question of Reincarnation*. McFarland.

Ian Stevenson, M.D. 2015. *European Cases Of The Reincarnation Type*. McFarland.

Ian Stevenson, M.D. 1997. *Where Reincarnation and Biology Intersect*. Praeger.

Raymond Moody. 2016. *Life After Life*. Ebury Digital.

Raymond Moody. 2013. *Glimpses of Eternity: Sharing a Loved One's Passage From This Lifetime to the Next*. Sakkara Productions.

Jim B. Tucker, M.D. 2013. *Return to Life: Extraordinary Cases of Children Who Remember Past Lives*. St Martin's Press.

Tom Shroder. 2001. *Old Souls: Compelling Evidence from Children Who Remember Past Lives*. Simon & Schuster.

Kevin J. Todeschi. 2008. *Edgar Cayce on The Akashic Records*. A.R.E. Press.

Edgar Cayce. 2018. *Edgar Cayce's Famous Black Book: An A-Z Guide to Cayce's Psychic Readings*. A.R.E. Press.

Recommended Reading: Metaphysics and the Nature of Consciousness

Dean Radin PhD. 2009. *The Conscious Universe: The Scientific Truth of Psychic Phenomena*. HarperOne.

Dean Radin PhD. 2006. *Entangled Minds: Extrasensory Experiences in a Quantum Reality*. Gallery Books.

Dean Radin PhD. 2018. *Real Magic: Ancient Wisdom, Modern Science, and a Guide to the Secret Power of the Universe*. Harmony.

Alan Ross Hugenot. 2016. *The New Science of Consciousness Survival and the Metaparadigm Shift to a Conscious Universe*. Dog Ear Publishing.

Gary E. Schwartz. 2011. *The Sacred Promise: How Science Is Discovering Spirit's Collaboration with Us in Our Daily Lives*. Atria Books/Beyond Words.

Russell Targ. 2012. *The Reality of ESP: A Physicist's Proof of Psychic Abilities*. Quest Books.

Chris Niebauer. 2019. *No Self, No Problem: How Neuropsychology Is Catching Up to Buddhism (The No Self Wisdom Series)*. Hierophant Publishing.

Recommended Reading: Leaving the Body

Robert Bruce. 2013. *The Treatise on Astral Projection: Director's Cut, V9*. Magic Light Press.

Robert A. Monroe. 1994. *Ultimate Journey*. Harmony.

William Buhlman. 1996. *Adventures Beyond the Body: How to Experience Out-of-Body Travel*. HarperOne.

William Buhlman. 2013. *Adventures in The Afterlife*. CreateSpace Independent Publishing Platform.

D. Scott Rogo. 2008. *Leaving the Body, A Complete Guide to Astral Projection*. Atria Books.

Recommended Reading: Zen and Buddhism

Alan Watts. 2021. *The Way of Zen*. Ebury Digital.

Alan Watts. 2011. *The Book on the Taboo Against Knowing Who You Are*. Souvenir Press.

Emma Slade. 2017. *Set Free: A Life-Changing Journey from Banking to Buddhism in Bhutan*. Summersdale Publishers Ltd

Recommended Reading: Develop Your Powers

William Buhlman and Susan Buhlman. 2016. *Higher Self Now!: Accelerating Your Spiritual Evolution*. www.astralinfo.org.

Henry Reed PhD. 1996. *Awakening Your Psychic Powers: Open Your Inner Mind and Control Your Psychic Intuition Today (Edgar Cayce Guides)*. St. Martin's Paperbacks.

Forbes Robbins Blair. 2004. *Instant Self-Hypnosis: How to Hypnotize Yourself with Your Eyes Open (35 Scripts for Reducing Stress, Anxiety, and Bad Habits)*. Sourcebooks.

Napoleon Hill. 2008. *The Law of Success: The Master Wealth-Builder's Complete and Original Lesson Plan for Achieving Your Dreams*. TarcherPerigee.

Charlie Morley. 2013. *Dreams of Awakening: Lucid Dreaming and Mindfulness of Dream and Sleep*. Hay House UK.

Linda Howe. 2009. *How to Read the Akashic Records: Accessing the Archive of the Soul and Its Journey*. Sounds True.

Recommended Reading: Beyond the Earthly Plane

Dolores Cannon. *The Convoluted Universe: Books One to Five*. Ozark Mountain Publishing.
Dolores Cannon. 2011. *The Three Waves of Volunteers and the New Earth*. Ozark Mountain Publishing.
Michael Newton PhD. 2010. *Journey of Souls: Case Studies of Life Between Lives*. Llewellyn Publications.
Michael Newton PhD. 2010. *Destiny of Souls: New Case Studies of Life Between Lives*. Llewellyn Publications.
Robert Schwartz. 2010. *Your Soul's Plan: Discovering the Real Meaning of the Life You Planned Before You Were Born*. North Atlantic Books.

Bibliography

[i] Targ, Russell. *The Reality of ESP. A Physicist's Proof of Psychic Abilities.* Quest Books. 2012.

[ii] Gary E. Schwartz. *The Afterlife Experiments: Breakthrough Scientific Evidence of Life After Death* Atria Books. 2003.

[iii] Andrew Benson. 2023. *globalnews.ca.* Viewed 15.02.23. <https://globalnews.ca/news/9411516/alcohol-consumption-decline-gen-z/>

[iv] The Nutrition Source. 2018. *hsph.harvard.edu.* Viewed 15.02.23. <https://www.hsph.harvard.edu/nutritionsource/healthy-weight/diet-reviews/mediterranean-diet/>

[v] Zita West. Year Unknown. *zitawest.com.* Viewed 15.02.23. <https://www.zitawest.com/pages/five-day-fertility-detox/>

[vi] Michael Mosley. Year Unknown. michaelmosley.co.uk. Viewed 15.02.23. <http://www.michaelmosley.co.uk/books.html/>

[vii] Grant Tinsley, Ph.D., CSCS,*D, CISSN and Jillian Kubala, MS, RD. 2020. healthline.com. Viewed 15.02.23. <https://www.healthline.com/health/one-meal-a-day>

[viii] Lauren Silva. 2023. forbes.com. Viewed 15.02.23. <https://www.forbes.com/health/body/cbd-oil-benefits/>

[ix] Yoga With Adriene. YouTube. https://www.youtube.com/@yogawithadriene

[x] Forbes Robbins Blair. *Instant Self-Hypnosis: How to Hypnotize Yourself with Your Eyes Open (35 Scripts for Reducing Stress, Anxiety, and Bad Habits).* Sourcebooks. 2004.

[xi] Charlie Morley. Year Unknown. charliemorley.com. Viewed 15.02.23. <https://www.charliemorley.com/about-me>

[xii] Independent. 2019. independent.co.uk. Viewed 15.02.23. <https://www.independent.co.uk/arts-entertainment/books/features/thrill-of-the-chaste-the-truth-about-gandhi-s-sex-life-b1912595.html>

[xiii] The Washington Post. 2016. washingtonpost.com. Viewed 15.02.23. <https://www.washingtonpost.com/news/worldviews/wp/2015/02/25/why-to-many-critics-mother-teresa-is-still-no-saint/>

[xiv] Mark E. Moore. 2022. biblestudytools.com. Viewed 15.02.23. <https://www.biblestudytools.com/bible-study/topical-studies/5-times-jesus-got-angry.html>

www.ingramcontent.com/pod-product-compliance
Lightning Source LLC
LaVergne TN
LVHW051557070426
835507LV00021B/2627